THE VIEW FROM THE CHAIR

To My Family
With Love

Acknowledgments
I wish to thank my twenty-eight interviewees who so generously gave me their time and the benefit of their varied experience. I also wish to record my sincere thanks to Patricia Oliver for her unfailing support, enthusiasm and encouragement.

THE VIEW FROM THE CHAIR
The Art of Chairing Meetings

Consuelo O'Connor

A ZIRCON BOOK

THE VIEW FROM THE CHAIR
A Zircon Book

Copyright © 1994 Consuelo O'Connor

ISBN 0 9516472 1 0 Cloth Bound Edition
ISBN 0 9516472 2 9 Paper Bound Edition

Published in Ireland by Zircon Publishing Limited,
Scarriff Bridge, Ballivor, Co. Meath.

Designed and Typeset by

DOTS

Dublin Online Typographic Services,
3-5 Camden Place, Dublin 2.

Printed in Dublin by ColourBooks Ltd.,
105 Baldoyle Industrial Estate, Baldoyle, Dublin 13.

Jacket illustration by Tom Byrne.

Contents

Foreword

IT IS, PERHAPS, A MEASURE of the extent to which talented chairpersons are difficult to find that committees are held in such popular contempt. A group of the unfit, appointed by the unwilling, to do the unnecessary; a group who keep minutes and waste hours; a group set up to do in a week what one good man can do in an hour; a group who, individually, can do nothing but as a group can decide that nothing can be done – these are just some of the popular, cynical ways in which committees and committee members are seen. Yet the fact remains that these days it is difficult to get anything done without recourse to a committee. Often a way of ensuring that nothing is done is to set one up. Yet, sooner or later, virtually everyone is confronted by the challenge of having to chair a meeting – whether it be a family argument over where to go on holiday, a voluntary organisation on the best way to raise some funds or a golf club committee deciding on the suitability of an applicant for membership.

We live, or so we are told, in the era of lobby politics so there is a party, coterie or pressure group on all manner of subjects from Alzheimer's disease to the future of the Zoo, and every one of them requires someone to preside over, guide, cajole, bully and persuade members over issues such as tactics, strategy, policy and principles. Yet, to date and thankfully, there are no schools of chairmanship laying down the law, insisting on necessary qualifications and jealously guarding their right to say who should or should not be allowed to practise. And so, by definition, the various chairpersons interviewed in this intriguing collection are all self-taught. They learned it on the job. Some started early – Olivia O'Leary chairing a debate at her convent school, Tony O'Reilly his school's Junior Cup rugby team – some left it very much later – Michael Smurfit and Ellen Mongon being well into adulthood when they first chaired the very different AGMs of Smurfits and the St Brigid's Travellers Women's Group respectively. Some clearly love the wheeling and dealing while others chafe at the limitations being in the chair places on their freedom to express their own opinions. Some work assiduously beforehand, sounding out positions, checking the mood, preparing the agenda, while others admit to playing it by ear and taking it as it comes. Nevertheless, there is a remarkable degree of consensus between them as to what constitutes a good chairman or chairwoman.

The Irish, suggests Peter Sutherland, may be particularly skilled because of our "natural ability" as communicators. This ability to communicate is repeatedly stressed by contributors as crucial to the art of chairmanship. In addition to the ability to manipulate language, an Irish characteristic if ever there was one, it encompasses the talent and the willingness to listen even to the most inveterate, narcissistic windbag intent on displaying mastery of the obvious. It includes a patience bordering on the saintly, crucial if viewpoints of diverse kinds and held with seeming obduracy are ever to be reconciled. It embraces the virtue of attentiveness. Chairing a meeting requires intense concentration if only to establish the hidden agenda which so many of the contributors identify as a feature of committee life from the GAA to GATT, from the League of Credit Unions to Europe's Council of Ministers.

But the good chairperson is more than a good communicator. There is the question of balance. On the one hand there is the need to be patient. On the other hand, time, as all of these busy people make clear, is precious or rather, as the more business oriented put it, costs money. Of course consensus must be sought but not if it takes too long. By all means listen to the long-winded, those suffering in Tony O'Reilly's words "a dose of the predictabilities", but at some point you must gently but firmly remind them of the need to spend time economically. Certainly display the empathy, caring and genuineness of a Californian holistic guru but make sure you run it through with a core of steel. Chairpersons are there to get things done. Do indeed display humour, grace, charm and charisma but, and this is an important caveat, resist the temptation to please everyone. Being a good chairperson, like so much else in life, means that not everyone will like you. Reconciling differences, seeking consensus, taking soundings, listening patiently – the good chairperson, as detailed by the contributors to this book, would appear to require the combined skills of a professional psychotherapist, a Hollywood actress, and a world-class chess player. In fact, as the contributors are at pains to point out, obeying a few basic rules sees you around most of the pitfalls. Display confidence, be humourous, do not box people into a corner and do not be irritable.

There is a consensus too about the bad chairperson. He or she does not listen but instead talks too much, badgers the group to arrive at a premature decision or endlessly procrastinates, is over-assertive to the point of bullying or exhibits the modesty of a Carthusian monk.

Contained within the pages of this book is much wisdom and much honesty too. Mary Harney certainly rings a bell with me when she suggests that the main disadvantage of being in the chair is that you have to stay relatively quiet. Tony O'Reilly may shake a few boardroom heads with his admission that he does not always arrive at meetings thoroughly prepared. Olivia O'Leary confesses to the occasional sin of brushing up on her notes when someone is making a point. Frank O'Kane identifies a quick temper and a tendency to sarcasm as his primary shortcomings. The point of all this self-criticism is surely to remind us that every chairman, even the most tried and tested, is not perfect. To chair a meeting requires such a cocktail of communication skills and personal qualities that the most we can aspire to is to do the best we can when called upon to do it.

Do women make better chairpersons than men? I am reminded of the story of the Australian insurance company that decided in the interests of reducing stress amongst its executives to hold some group meetings involving the executives and their spouses. Ostensibly to assist the spouses to help reduce executive stress, the meetings instead revealed to the company the untapped well of skills possessed by the spouses regarding such issues as time management, problem solving, consensus reaching and conflict resolution. They were to a woman (and the majority were women) exceedingly well endowed with the kind of abilities that management consultancy firms have made fortunes out of teaching in a systematic way to thousands of executives around the world. The answer is not difficult to find. In organising a home, balancing the conflicting needs of self, spouse, children of varying ages, relationships, time and feelings, women have had to develop all sorts of skills and have done so over generations. For what it is worth, my experience is that women make excellent chairpersons because for most of them listening comes much more naturally than it does to men, resolving conflict is part of their everyday world and not just something they attend to in the workplace and being conscious of the 'hidden agenda', what feelings lie behind the spoken word or the confusing action, is the *sine qua non* of family life. Now there is a debate I would be willing to chair – after reading this book thoroughly once again!

Anthony Clare.

Introduction

WATCHING BOTH effective and incompetent chairing of meetings over many years led me, some time ago, to ask myself what the key elements were that led to one or the other. Why was it that some meetings seemed to flow along effortlessly, in a controlled and cordial manner, with everyone making a contribution and wise decisions being taken, while others were disorganised, fractious and inconclusive? What special skills were required, what personality traits were most valuable in a competent chairperson? I began to observe more closely the conduct of chairmen and chairwomen at every meeting I attended. I asked colleagues for their views and I came, not unexpectedly, to the conclusion that those who had experience of actually being in the chair themselves had the most insight into the 'art of chairing meetings'. Everyone, however, had an opinion and I began to see that the topic was one which could be of interest to a wider audience. I decided to ask a cross section of people, who might be expected to know, what the tricks of the trade were. I chose people I knew well and people I had never met before (my style of referring to them reflects this). I chose people who operate in the professional world and those who give their services voluntarily. I included politics and sport, culture and business, trade unionism and religion, men and women. I looked for those with a great deal of experience and those with relatively little. The result is a group of twenty-eight people in Irish society who tell us, in their own individual ways, how they tackle the important task of chairing meetings.

How to describe the role, now that more and more women are chairing meetings, presented an interesting problem. I prefer to use "chairman" and "chairwoman" when the sex is known and to use "chairperson" only when it is not, as for instance in "a chairperson will be elected. . . " It seems ridiculous to me to use "chairman" when it is a man and "chairperson" when it is a woman. I have, however, chosen to use the language of the interviewee throughout.

We live in an age in which communications technology has exploded. Fax, mobile telephones and e-mail are common, tele-conferences can be held while participants sit in their own offices. Nevertheless, these are rarely a substitute for what can be achieved by people sitting down in a room together at a meeting. There, body language can be observed, human contact is established and most importantly (according to many of the people in this book) humour can be shared.

Finally, I found it particularly fascinating that one of Ireland's most famous businessmen should cite "charm" as a particularly desirable attribute in a chairperson. I can certainly testify that all of my interviewees were most charming to me.

Consuelo O'Connor
Dublin, November 1994.

Chapter 1

Jack Boothman

JACK BOOTHMAN describes his style of chairmanship as laid back. He sees himself as captain of a team and stresses the importance of team work. With over two thousand GAA clubs around the country, a staff at Croke Park of fifteen, and forty members on the Central Council of the GAA, the team he chairs is a large one but he is modest about this. "I feel I am just a captain of a team who is running the association. But I am not in a position of power. I never have been. I think power is a loser. I try to get away from it. The smallest little school child comes up to me and says 'hello Jack'. Perhaps there is some prestige attached to the job, I don't know."

All his experience of chairing is in the voluntary arena but he has a professional approach to the job and he expects others to be the same. "When I talk about professionalism I refer to the quality of work. We are not paid but that shouldn't take away from the quality of our work. I wouldn't accept amateur work. It is voluntary work but it has to be of a professional level. The fact that you pay people does not necessarily mean that you are going to get a better quality of work. It does give you the advantage or disadvantage that you are able to fire people if they are paid but in our organisation you can't do that."

Being the leader of a large voluntary organisation involves being able to bring people along with you. "I think that is probably the most important part of being a chairman. You won't get far by being a dictator. Nor will you get very far by driving people. And the sergeant-major approach, the army approach, won't work in everyday life. It isn't necessarily very efficient either. You could get decisions and finish a meeting in twenty minutes but if you leave ten very disgruntled people behind you when you take up your papers and walk out of a room that is not doing the Association any good either."

So he urges his committee members, cajoles them and makes them work. "I like to be on a committee where everybody works. Too many committees

"The cup of tea interlude serves the same purpose as taking a three week break."

depend on the chairman and expect him to do all the work. I like to see all the committee having an input and also working in between meetings. I would arrange for some members of the committee to look up or research certain projects and report back to a future meeting."

Jack says that, while a chairman might go into a meeting with firm views on certain matters, he must have an open mind. "You may not achieve the ideal. Other people are entitled to have good ideas. I find that most people, not just me, don't necessarily examine the opposing point of view. In your mind you are making only one side of the argument. I believe your mind has to be open to what in political terms are called amendments. In the political arena you can sense when a minister is in fear of losing face. He or she will refuse to take on board the opposition's amendments. And the party votes blindly against the opposition. You don't see many amendments getting through even though they might appear to be quite good to the neutral observer."

Once a decision is taken by the Central Council of the GAA everybody on that committee is bound by it and no one is at liberty to go and speak against it publicly. And again he draws an analogy with government. "It is something like cabinet responsibility. You can't have any discipline or order in an organisation if people feel they can go off to do their own thing."

When a meeting is very divided on an important subject Jack thinks it is often advisable to delay taking a decision. People can then reflect on the matter and often more information comes to light. "The trouble is that you often don't have all the information and things can change. If it is a long meeting we usually break for a cup of tea and that can be very useful. There is informal discussion. Things can be thrashed out and you can come up with a formula. You will find it easier then to get a decision when you go back to the meeting. The cup of tea interlude serves the same purpose as taking a three week break."

Jack believes the skills needed to be a good chairman can be learned, though this may take some years of hard work and practice. He intends to introduce training courses in the GAA on how to take decisions, keep minutes and apply the rules of the organisation correctly. "I am a great admirer of Macra na Feirme, which is a rural-based organisation, and they have produced many great leaders. They believe in leadership courses and I hope to introduce them in the GAA. The skills I would have taught are the same skills needed to run a small business. Of course, you could be taught every skill in the business and, at the end of the day, you may not be a good chairman. You need to be even-tempered. Although, you know, most high powered executives who get to the top are probably not even-tempered. A chairman must always remember that there are human beings out there in front of him, people with problems, personal problems, and in our organisation they are giving their time freely to help out. You have to treat them with respect. And remember that even the most important decision is not earth-shattering. People attach too much importance in life to their own ability or to their own position in life and they think that when they make a decision it is going to change the whole world. But the world has been around for a long time and our association has been around for a hundred and ten years and it is still motoring along. It is not a matter of life or death."

If Jack had an unusual or innovative idea he would pick up the phone to talk to a few people about it before the meeting. He feels it is better if every original idea is not seen to come from the chair. "I would probably discuss the idea with the secretary long before the meeting. I am a great man for consulting people. And then I would talk to the people who are most vocal and likely to voice opposition. I would talk to them in a general way. It is amazing when you do this they will come up later with the same idea as you had. They think it is their idea and then you are away in a hack. You have to do this man management, the political side, the stroking, the cajoling, if you want to get things done. That is the way the world is run. There is no such thing as objectivity. Everybody has a hidden agenda and you have to find out what the hidden agenda is and play on that."

Jack hates to see time wasted and does not have discussions about facts. "Facts are facts. There is no use arguing about facts. It is a waste of time. Life is too

"Too many committees depend on the chairman and expect him to do all the work."

short and I haven't time to waste. What is important is the implication of the fact and how it will affect the decision you are going to make."

He believes that a poor chairman is the one who tries to be all things to all people, someone who tries to be nice to everybody, and he says that a chair needs to have a core of steel. "People on the floor of a meeting sense very quickly a weak chairman whom they can twist around their little finger and that is bad. People are not stupid, they are very shrewd and a fellow will speak once, twice or three times. And the weak chairman will let him do that."

Jack Boothman is President of the Gaelic Athletic Association. He is a veterinary surgeon and has served as Chairman of the Leinster Council of the GAA 1988-1991; Wicklow Leinster Council Representative 1982-1985; Chairman of Youth Development 1982-1984; Secretary/Chairman of the Blessington GAA Club 1982-1987 and Vice Chairman of the Wicklow County Board of the GAA 1969-1972.

Chapter 2

Gillian Bowler

GILLIAN BOWLER is very impatient about wasting time – both her own and other people's. "I loathe wasting time and I get irritated if people have not read the documents relating to a meeting. I do not mind people having their share in a debate on a strategic issue but when they waste time on something that is simple, minor and petty then this always annoys me and I tend to get tough."

In fact, Gillian thinks it is important in a competent chairman to have the ability to be tough though, she says, this may be her impatient nature coming through. "And you have to be thoroughly disciplined in the control of meetings. You run them efficiently and commercially. To me, that is the number one rule."

The role of chairman is, she says, "to be leading, motivating and good for strategic planning". Sometimes she likes to throw the fat in the fire, stir things up, in order to promote a constructive tension which releases more ideas.

As well as running her own travel business Gillian Bowler has, over the years, sat on committees and chaired many business and voluntary bodies. "I don't think voluntary chairmanships are any different from any other kind. You are there to do a job and you do it to the best of your ability." However, she says that it is important to be more prepared for these voluntary meetings. "There is more homework involved in being a non-executive chairman in the sense that one isn't easily comfortable or knowledgeable about the role, so there is a learning process. There is one huge difference, of course. I get paid in commercial life. Apart from that important fact there is no difference. I am very hard-headed commercially. Everything I have done in my life I have done for the purpose of making money in the end."

Gillian sees the relationship between the chairman and chief executive as very important and says that she has been very lucky in this area. "If the relationship is bad it makes it very difficult to progress board matters. I think the secret is to work and to give full support to the chief executive. But you have to be rewarded in the sense that the chief executive in turn has to be good at his job." Gillian is currently part-time non-executive Chairman of the Museum of Modern Art at Kilmainham Hospital, and spends time every day working on it. She often spends a day there with the chief executive. "It is a joint role. You have to be prepared to put in the time with each other. As a non-executive chairman one has to know as much about the facts and figures as one does in one's own company. One relies on the chief executive, but also on the other senior management staff."

She does not find it difficult any longer to exercise authority at meetings, but admits that this is something which used to worry her more than anything else. "Every chairman on every board will have somebody who wants to contribute too much, who will talk for half an hour on any topic and who has a view on every subject, including the purchase of ball-point pens. You just have to cut across people and say 'we have debated this long enough, we don't have any more time, thank you for your contribution'. The problem is when that person keeps coming back to the subject and won't be shut up. I think at that stage one has to be almost rude and say enough is enough."

Gillian Bowler would not 'manage' in the sense of getting support for a line of action in advance of the meeting.

"But I might, for example, divide work into sub-committees so that action is faster. If a financial matter was coming up, I would contact the chairman of the finance committee and tell him I needed a paper covering this point. And if there was a contentious matter coming up, I would announce this at the previous board meeting and ask them to notify me if they want to speak. In this way, I can plan in advance. But I certainly don't canvass votes or count votes in advance, no."

On one occasion only that she can remember Gillian found the board going in a direction with which she was not at all in agreement. "But I felt it was important not to wade in first with my opinion so I held back a bit. The board found it quite difficult because there were strong feelings on both sides. And

"I don't think voluntary chairmanships are any different from any other kind."

"I loathe wasting time and I get irritated if people have not read the documents relating to a meeting."

my own feelings were quite strong but strength of them and said I was open to arg the end the board was 60/40 in favour of the way she felt, but not until there had been a long and tortuous discussion. Gillian tends to see both sides of an argument, which she finds difficult. "I think it is the role of a chairman not to enforce his own opinion. There should be a democratic majority decision." However, if there was a decision with which she was totally in disagreement, she would minute her dissociation from the decision. "I would not expose myself to defending a course of action which I thought was totally and ethically wrong." Gillian, like many others, works mostly by consensus. In fact, she remembers only one occasion in a voluntary committee having to take a vote and the matter under discussion was not of great importance. A complete impasse rarely occurs at her meetings. She has a clear mind and if she sees trouble ahead she focuses on why it is there. She often finds that getting more information can help to solve the problem. "In a complete impasse I might leave the matter to the next board meeting and look for more information to support either argument."

Gillian finds that, by and large, directors in a commercial company usually have a very valuable input, even if they only speak occasionally. "One doesn't want somebody on the board who has got an opinion on everything all the time." She finds state boards more difficult. Perhaps 90% of the members pull their weight. "And then one is faced with a 10% who either never turn up, turn up rarely or who don't say anything at all at the meetings. Then I try to get an opinion from them. Or I give them a specific task to do rather like a school teacher, and frankly if that doesn't work after three or four goes I give up."

Gillian has also come across some very poor chairmen and has strong views on this subject. "The single worst fault is somebody who is totally undisciplined and who lets people speak haphazardly all over the place without following an agenda. Total confusion reigns. The second most intolerable fault, which is equally as bad as the first, is somebody who ignores totally the board and its agenda. They work to their own secret agenda. They make deals in secret, make deals on the phone and produce minutes which bear no relation to what transpired at a previous meeting. And they ignore the wishes of other board members to such an extent that they wonder why they are on the board in the first place. This kind of dictatorial chairman says effectively 'we won't all discuss this because I have done this, this and this'. Really, why does anybody serve on this kind of board?"

However, Gillian does not tolerate this kind of chairman. "One can always resign, but I feel this is somewhat defeatist. No, I would fight back and say 'excuse me, that is not what we agreed at the last meeting. It is clear to me we agreed such and such. I don't think this can be passed over, I want to discuss it. My understanding is that the majority of the board are of a different view from you'. Usually other board members will support you, though they might not have been willing to bring up the matter themselves."

Gillian likes to start meetings on time, and says that in Ireland this is always an issue. She likes morning meetings. "My own experience is that people start to flag from mid afternoon. We get their best thoughts in the morning. After office hours I don't think people are at their best."

She does not approve of big, three-course lunches and has, in fact, abolished them on one committee which she chairs. Instead, they have sandwiches and coffee and they eat as they work. It all comes back to not wasting time.

While she does not want to take on additional work at the moment, Gillian enjoys the role of chairman. She admits that she likes running things. She is currently serving on another board "but I find myself itching to take over. I am essentially bossy by nature."

She chaired her first meeting in England when she was sixteen. This was running a dance at the local town hall. "I certainly wasn't intimidated. I don't think I have ever been intimidated. I knew what I wanted to achieve so I didn't have any self-conscious feelings about doing it." Her advice to someone chairing meetings for the first time is "the same advice that applies to anything you do in life, do your homework, be well prepared,

"I would not expose myself to defending a course of action which I thought was totally and ethically wrong."

have a clear view of what you want to achieve. Don't let people waffle or say nothing. Set the agenda, have a rough idea of the time span and be fair."

Gillian Bowler is Managing Director of Budget Travel Ltd. She sold her company to Granada plc in 1987. She is currently a Director of Granada Travel. She is also a board member Independent Radio & Television Commission; Chairman Irish Museum of Modern Art at Kilmainham; Member of Australia/Ireland Economic Committee; Director of Leisure World; Director of Temple Bar Properties; Director of Temple Bar Renewal Ltd., Chairman of the Special Traffic Development Task Force for Shannon Airport; Director Spring Grove Services; Director Institute of Directors of Ireland. Previously she was a Board Member Irish Goods Council; Chairman of Tourism Task Force; Chairman Dublin Heritage Area Development Group; Board Member of Douglas Hyde Gallery. She is former chairman of the Tour Operators Council and former chairman of the National Council of Irish Travel Agents Association. A Director of the Irish Cancer Society and a Member of the Marketing Institute of Ireland, Gillian Bowler was awarded a Doctor of Law Honoris Causa in 1989 from the National Council of Education. She is also a committee member of various charitable organisations.

Chapter 3

Harold Clarke

HAROLD CLARKE readily admits that he likes the power of being Chairman of Easons which employs over eight hundred people. One senses that he runs a very tight ship. Board meetings take place once a month and he starts them on the stroke of 10.45 am *always*. All board members know each other very well and every decision is arrived at by consensus. He points out that never in the hundred year history of Easons has a vote ever taken place. For him, preparation is the name of the game.

He sees his fourteen member board as being a very large one compared to many other companies. In addition to their formal monthly meetings, all directors who are in Dublin meet informally every morning over coffee. In this way, he knows the views which are emerging before they ever come before the board. Papers are, of course, circulated in advance of meetings. In some instances he circulates just one copy to board members inviting them to write their views on it. This then comes back to him before a meeting and he is therefore aware of views which are emerging. "We all know each other's minds very well so we don't have to declare in so many words what our views are. When I go into a board meeting I can virtually tell what the views of everybody there will be." No minutes are circulated. They only record decisions and these are read out by the company secretary at the start of the meeting.

Harold Clarke became Chairman of Easons in 1986 and enjoys the role. He says that the adrenalin flows faster before a meeting. "But I hope it would, because once you started to take board meetings casually you would cease to make a worthwhile contribution to the company." If a meeting starts to go wrong this would probably be the result of inadequate preparation. In that case he would either let the discussion flow until a consensus was arrived at. Or, he says, "the classic thing to do is appoint a sub-committee – and there probably isn't any other better way – because it allows people time to think."

He likes to get decisions taken and if the board fails to do this he regards this to be a result of inadequate preparation, inadequate lobbying, inadequate talking. He believes that directors' time is far too precious and they are too highly paid to have fourteen people discussing what could be discussed by two or three people in a committee. He likes to draw out the more silent or reserved members of the board and encourages the "weaker brethren" to make their contribution. He says that all boards have people who talk too much but he has his own way of dealing with this problem and thinks he is quite effective. He simply says "Yes, John, I know your view – I'd like to hear David's."

Harold Clarke thinks a chairman *has* to be detached if he is to be effective. "That is the great merit of not having the same person as chairman and managing director within a company. The chairman can take 'a slightly more distant view of problems and he can support directors by being a little removed'." As to who is the leader in a company, he says it depends on the personnel within the company. It depends on the sort of business a company is running, the level of intelligence, the level of commitment. The chairman could be a catalyst or "a sort of traffic controller". Either way, the chairman must support his managing director. In his case he has a close personal and business relationship with his managing director but recognises that in some companies a more distant relationship works better.

The one time a board meeting went off the rails for him was, he readily admits, due to his lack of preparation. "It was all my fault. It always comes back to preparation. When people started to disagree with a proposal I had put they were absolutely correct. My proposal was an incorrect one."

"...once you started to take board meetings casually you would cease to make a worthwhile contribution to the company."

He says a poor chairman is one who has imprecise goals. A bad chairman fails to bring everyone into the discussion. And a boring chairman kills all interest. "It is very important to be non-boring as a chairman." The competent chairman always has a clear

"It is very important to be non-boring as a chairman."

objective. "In business the idea is always to make money." Having a clear brain is important, as is enthusiasm. "Try to inspire people if you can. Charisma is not something you can learn very easily but you get a feeling that you can inspire people into action by using the correct words."

He cites the late Lord Rosse with whom he served on the Friends of the National Collection as being a brilliant chairman, wonderfully articulate and always with very clear goals. "He sometimes steamrolled his views through, but you always felt that the meeting was effective."

To those starting out he says "the first thing to do is to listen. Then learn to summarise, because meetings can get very confused and convoluted. Learn to summarise in twenty words what has taken five hundred words of discussion."

He himself first became a chairman when aged twenty-one. This was of the Student Representative Council of TCD. He readily admits to wanting to be Chairman of Easons and goes on to say "Funnily enough, I didn't want to be managing director and obviously my colleagues didn't want me to be either because they did not appoint me. I enjoy the particular form of leadership you get when you are chairman." Two hours, he says, is the ideal and outside length of time for a meeting; after that people lose their concentration. Chairing a board meeting is quite tiring for him and he breathes a sigh of relief when he is at the end of Any Other Business.

Harold makes the point that there is no place where you can train to be a competent chairman. Some people are, he feels, thrown in at the deep end and he takes as an example the bishop. "He becomes a priest and may end up as a bishop having to chair diocesan meetings with no training whatsoever."

Inspiring confidence in the company is also a very important function for Harold Clarke. "I regard that as one of the most important parts of the chairman's job. The public relations image he projects is vital. If he is strong on integrity he will inspire confidence in the company."

Harold Clarke is Chairman of Eason & Son Limited. Born in Roscommon he was educated at The King's Hospital, Dublin and TCD (Moderator in Economic and Political Science, MA). He joined Easons in 1954, becoming a ·Director in 1968 and Chairman in 1986. He is the author of Ireland in Colour *(1970);* Georgian Dublin *(1972);* The Splendour of Ireland *(1976) and has contributed to various books and periodicals on conservation and the arts. He is President of the Friends of the National Collections of Ireland and a member of the Christ Church Cathedral Board.*

Chapter 4

Dr Brendan Comiskey, Bishop of Ferns

THE BISHOP OF FERNS, Dr Brendan Comiskey, describes his style of chairmanship as a benign dictatorship. However, he avoids chairing meetings where there are lay people present. "A bishop shouldn't chair a meeting if there are going to be lay people at it. He should get someone else to chair it. A lot of lay people will defer too much to the chair if the bishop is in it. There is too much awe and a feeling that the 'bishop knows what he is talking about' even if this is not so."

Dr Comiskey is from Co. Monaghan and is one of only two Irish bishops who are members of a religious congregation, the Sacred Hearts Congregation, which he entered in 1954. He received a licentiate in Theology from the Lateran University and also studied moral theology in Rome. He has lectured in moral theology in the US, was elected Provincial Superior of the Anglo-Irish province of his order in 1971 and subsequently became Secretary-General of the Conference of Major Religious Superiors. He also studied management in TCD and graduated in 1979 with an MSc.

Dr Comiskey believes in going into a meeting with some kind of a proposal to put on the table if only so that it will be amended, improved or displaced by a completely different proposal. He feels his approach gives a shape or form to a meeting which otherwise "just becomes endless talk".

Like many other people he has suffered from poorly chaired meetings. "The poorest chair is the one who has no idea of where the meeting is coming from, where it is going, what it hopes to achieve, what he hopes to be different, what changes he hopes to bring about. He doesn't believe in the purpose of the meeting in the first place and his sole goal is to survive the two hours of its duration."

He attended many meetings when he lived abroad and finds that many Europeans have a very different approach from ours. "For example if there were Spaniards at the meetings they would usually be quite chaotic... now the

"...nobody ever went away from a meeting ...feeling that they did not have their say, and that is very important."

Belgians would be more like us. The Italians would be Italian, the meetings would go all over the place – it was great fun but lacking in discipline."

"Another feature was that they would talk endlessly about totally impractical things." However, the Bishop went on to say tactfully that these experiences were over ten years ago and he thought the EC would have helped to improve things.

It seems that the Bishops' Conference at Maynooth is a fairly relaxed meeting, although it lasts three days. About six years ago all the bishops went 'apart' and had a separate meeting in Swords for a week with a view to improving the format and procedures of the regular hierarchical meeting. "We met for a week and we drew up an extensive list of resolutions and improvements and in the end we never implemented a single one of them." The agenda for the Maynooth meeting looks very structured and formal but the meeting is very relaxed and tends to wander from time to time.

They start with a prayer, end with a prayer, have Mass on the first evening and they are joined by the Papal Nuncio. Dr Comiskey says that they are like any ordinary meeting of Irish men, not unduly reverential or polite. Some take it more seriously than others, some talk too little, some too much. "It is very hard to shut up a bishop, you know." The difference between these thirty-six men and thirty-six business men is, however, that a bishop can decide not to implement in his own diocese the decisions arrived at in Maynooth. "The boys can go home and they need not implement a single thing decided on. They are bosses in their own territories. As Pope Leo XIII once said, when somebody talked about the Irish bishops, 'there are no bishops in Ireland, there are twenty-six popes'."

Bishop Comiskey says that matters such as people falling away from the Church do not necessarily weigh heavily on their deliberations or discussions at these meetings. "I think young people always fell away from the Church. The big question which has to be answered in this generation is will they come back? We have a lot of competition in the environment – different churches preaching different messages to the young. I don't think we should get into a tail spin provided we are doing our work and preaching the gospel and, above all, trying to live it and be good humoured, tolerant and kind... we should teach by our behaviour and our composure. If we teach hopelessness, pessimism and rigid conservatism and if we have not found the joy of Christ in our own lives, then we cannot just automatically presume that we are the right teachers or teaching the right things. It has been said, and I believe this, that the Church has the right answers but is using the wrong language."

Dr Comiskey finds the Maynooth meetings long but very enjoyable nonetheless. Some of his colleagues hate them. The late Bishop Birch dreaded them so much that he used to count the days between them. Cardinal Daly is, says Dr Comiskey, a very good chairman, whereas the late Cardinal O Fiaich was not. "He was so interested in people that he became fascinated by them even if they were talking nonsense. He was overly people orientated and he would not move the meeting forward but then nobody ever went away from a meeting back to their diocese feeling that they did not have their say, and that is very important."

When Dr Comiskey chairs a meeting he would not do any lobbying beforehand because he feels this would be seen as loading the meeting. However if another bishop were in the chair Dr Comiskey wouldn't hesitate to try to enlist support for something he felt strongly about. If his line is supported by three or four people then he feels he will have more chance of success, "otherwise it could look as if Comiskey is just talking off the top of his head".

The Bishop says that in exercising authority a chairman should do this with great good humour and enormous tolerance. And, he says, the worst thing a chairman can do is to put someone down at a meeting because this will be a pyrrhic victory. "If you cut in on someone or get them to shut up not only have you created an enemy but you have created a zone of hostility where three or four of his or her friends don't like the way the chair has ruled and will be far more intent on getting one over on you than in trying to accomplish something."

...the worst thing a chair can do is to put someone down at a meeting...

"There is nothing like a six o'clock train."

If a meeting comes to an impasse and there appears to be no way forward the Bishop would move on to the next topic. Then he would come back to the original point at the end of the meeting when everyone is very tired and they would, he says, push nearly anything through in order to get home. "There is nothing like a six o'clock train."

In his view women on a committee make the same kind of input as men. When working in the Conference of Major Religious Superiors he was told frequently to expect a different type of contribution from women but this did not turn out to be so. "I have never perceived any great difference between the contributions women make and men make. Some men make terrible contributions, some women make terrible contributions. And there are some masculine women and feminine men." He says that the women he deals with are confident and articulate.

With very loquacious committee members Dr Comiskey usually lets them speak once at great length until they exhaust themselves and then they are usually quite happy. "If they keep on interrupting after that I note the other five, six or seven people who have indicated they want to speak and I call out their names... by the time they have finished speaking the talkative person won't bother trying to come in again."

With regard to silent people at a meeting Dr Comiskey doesn't try to draw them out. He finds it more difficult to deal with people who go in for pregnant silences and who thereby try to torpedo the meeting. "I'm talking about the person who is seething with rage, energy and unhappiness. They use non-verbal communication and body language to communicate disagreement or dissatisfaction with the meeting, and the way it is being chaired and the decisions being reached, but they say nothing. Usually they are not happy with themselves. They seethe and groan and usually I do not call on them to speak. I let them seethe and groan because they are trying to control the meeting. Actually, they are trying to get love and affection for themselves. It's a personal problem coming up in a meeting."

The Bishop feels that the chairman can make a great contribution to the organisation he is serving. But, paradoxically, he sees it as a weak position. He says one is better off not being in the chair if one holds strong views or wants to speak vigorously on a subject, "A good chairman can get the best out of people. But if you speak vigorously from the chair you put people off. But it might be different in the business world."

His advice to people who are chairing a meeting for the first time is to prepare well in order to be confident within oneself. A chairman should closely observe the people at a meeting and make sure that people who want to speak are called upon. "And don't defer too much to other people just because you are young. That's nonsense, either you are in the chair or you are out of the chair."

Bishop Brendan Comiskey became Bishop of Ferns in May 1984. He is a member of the National Episcopal Conference, Chairman of the Bishops' Commission for Communications and President of the Catholic Communications Institute of Ireland. He is also a member of the Bishops' Commissions for Ecumenism and Education; the Joint Commission of Bishops and Religious Superiors and the Commission for Youth. He is a member of the Glenstal Ecumenical Conference. He is Chairman of the Irish Churches' Council for Television and Radio Affairs (ICCTRA). Bishop Comiskey was ordained to the priesthood in the Congregation of the Sacred Hearts at Tanagh, Co. Monaghan in 1961. He pursued post-graduate studies in Theology as well as in the Classics at the Catholic University of America and the Lateran University in Rome. In 1969 he was elected Provincial of the Anglo-Irish province of the Congregation of the Sacred Hearts and Secretary-General of the Conference of Major Religious Superiors in 1974. In November 1979 he was named Auxiliary Bishop of Dublin. In the same month he graduated with an MSc from Trinity College, Dublin, the first Catholic bishop ever to graduate from there. On 20 January 1980 he was ordained bishop at St Andrew's, Westland Row, Dublin. Bishop Comiskey is a Patron of the Wexford Festival Opera and was made a Freeman of Wexford Town in June 1990.

Chapter 5

Liam Connellan

LIAM CONNELLAN sees himself as a chairman who listens. "Listening is a very important part of the chairman's role. He has to get the mood of the meeting, weigh up the views of the members and then guide the meeting towards a satisfactory conclusion. A chairman has to have vision, to know where he is trying to bring the organisation and to try to lead it there. One usually goes to a meeting with particular objectives which one wants to achieve."

Currently Chairman of a large state board – The National Roads Authority – which has a budget of *c.* £200m. per year, he says that there he operates within a broad strategy which has been developed by Government. "In a state organisation one has to be much more aware of Government policy. The focus is to make sure there is good value for money and that things are prioritised in the right way. The first thing I have to do is to ensure that the fourteen members operate as a board, as a unified group rather than as representatives. This is done by having an ever deeper understanding of what the issues are. The board members have a responsibility to the Government, to the state. They come from very different backgrounds and this is extremely valuable because it means no key issue will be left unconsidered."

Liam sees no fundamental difference in being in the chair of a commercial enterprise, a state board or a voluntary organisation. "There are many common elements between the three in terms of developing the collegiality of a board and they are working together for the good of the organisation. For example, I am chairman of a venture capital fund, the Smurfit Job Creation Enterprise Fund, and there the goals are very precise. We have clear objectives. We then have to put the resources in place – both marketing and operational resources – to ensure the objectives can be achieved. That applies to other organisations also. So, the distinctions may be more apparent than real between the different types of organisations."

"...a poor chair is one who talks too much and who does not get decisions."

Liam also has experience of running a voluntary organisation as Director General of the Confederation of Irish Industry. "I ran a voluntary organisation for twenty years. Members joined annually and paid a subscription. One has to be very aware of the views of members in a situation like that. One has to get the objectives clarified. A commercial organisation, it seems to me, can have a more unified direction – to grow and operate profitably. Members of a voluntary organisation may have a very wide variety of objectives and one has to put greater emphasis on communication with members. Also, one probably needs to be more patient."

In Liam's view, a poor chairman is one who talks too much and who does not get decisions. "A chair should listen and guide but not dominate the meeting. If someone talks too much and wants to impose his or her view on everybody else, that is not the mark of a good chairman. Sometimes people fall into that trap. If a chairman has ten items on the agenda and if after one and a half hours he is only at the end of item two, well, that is not very good. He should try to think through beforehand approximately how long each agenda item should take and divide up the meeting accordingly. People will have allocated a particular amount of time to attend the meeting so it is important to complete it on time. In most cases it should not go beyond one and a half hours or two hours maximum. After two hours people get tired, their attention wanders, they don't really participate or they lose focus."

If a total impasse emerged at a meeting in spite of thorough preparation, listening, guiding, moving things forward, Liam would postpone taking a decision if that were possible. He would then consult individually with board members, brief himself more fully and try to ascertain why there are differences of view. "Going through this process may change the views of members including those of the chairman. Sometimes I have found that the difference of views may be related simply to drafting issues, to the way something is said rather than opposition to its substance. Sometimes decisions have to be fudged a little. One develops a statement, a compromise statement, which may be preferable to not having a decision at all."

It is helpful if a chairman has a certain degree of authority and board members expect this quality in their chair. Authority comes from three sources, says Liam. The first is knowledge. "Knowledge gives authority. You can develop this by preparation, by knowing your subject. Then there is the authority people have just because they are in the chair, a structural authority. Most people when they attend a meeting recognise that the only way a meeting can be run effectively is by having the meeting run by the chairman. So they will defer to the chairman, and this automatically gives him a certain authority. They will say 'and with your permission may I ask so and so...' They avoid chit-chatting across the table. So this gives authority as well. It is quite interesting to see the way in which people will change a relationship with another person because they are in the chair. And then there is a third type of authority which is a personal authority and some people are fortunate in having the right kind of personality for the role, the ability to communicate in a certain way."

Liam stresses the point that the chairman is the leader. He is the leader of the team but it is a team. He needs to be open to ideas, to have a receptive attitude, because otherwise committee members are not inclined to come forward with ideas. "If committee members feel that the chairman is going to close them down rather rapidly the minute they open their mouth, that would be very bad for the collegiate nature of the board and for the way in which the board operates together. It is important that the chairman should be seen to be independent and even-handed." Liam would seek out the views of a silent member because it is vital that everybody should contribute to the discussion rather than have the views of any one person dominate. They are part of the team.

The role of non-executive board members is extremely important because of the independence and wide experience which they bring to a discussion. "It is amazing that while executives can be extraordinarily good in their own areas they can lack knowledge of the broader environment in which they operate. A board which is made up of executives can be really quite inward looking. They can suffer a lot. They can miss out

"In a state organisation one has to be much more aware of Government policy."

because of the fact that they get into tunnel vision and become unaware of solutions to some of their problems. Many people recommend that the majority of board members should be non-executive but this does not happen very often in small or medium sized companies. They miss out in growing and developing their company. The non-executive director can bring a wider vision to a company and they come *very, very* inexpensively."

To an inexperienced person, Liam's advice is to spend time on preparation. "The first thing to do is to construct the agenda carefully. Read all the board papers thoroughly. Ask yourself 'what do I want to achieve?' Think out how you will get everybody to contribute and see that no one dominates. Try to develop a tentative timetable for the meeting. Move it along. If one thinks about these things in advance, the chances of the meeting turning out quite well in the end will be greatly increased. As a famous golfer once said, 'I find that the more I practise the luckier I get'."

Liam Connellan is currently Chairman of The National Roads Authority; Chairman Smurfit Job Creation Enterprise Fund; Chairman Generale des Eaux Ireland; Chairman Irish American Partnership; Chairman The Boardroom Centre; Vice-President of the Royal Dublin Society and Chairman of its Industry Committee; Chairman Irish Construction Quality Assurance; Chairman Code Monitoring Committee for the Marketing of Infant Formulae; Deputy Chairman British Irish Industry Circle and Director Johnson & Higgins. He is a member of the Economic & Social Committee of European Communities; Council of Economic and Social Research Institute; Executive Committee Institute of European Affairs; Board of University Industry Centre, UCD; Committee of Friends of the Irish College in Paris. He has served on many Irish and European boards, councils and commissions; worked in the Irish Management Institute from 1965 to 1972 and was Director General of the Confederation of Irish Industry from 1972 to 1992. He was elected a Fellow of the Institution of Engineers of Ireland in 1982; an Honorary Member of the German-Irish Chamber of Industry and Commerce in 1982 and was awarded the Distinguished Cross of Merit (first class) of the Federal Republic of Germany in 1985.

Chapter 6

Desmond Fitz-Gerald, Knight of Glin

DESMOND FITZ-GERALD, KNIGHT OF GLIN, does not regard himself as an experienced chairman but he has, nonetheless, very definite views on the subject. He describes his style of chairmanship as "rather disorganised" and says he is not an organised person. "And I'm not good at allocating time."

He thinks it is important that a chairman should have a light touch, a sense of humour and "considerable force about not letting people meander too much". He believes in going around the table and trying to draw people out. "You should try to get their points of view, if they have any. Some people will say 'I pass on that one' but often the more silent people have more important things to say than the ones who talk too much. A chairman should have the ability to sum up and to ask 'is this what you really mean?' And then people either shut up or rephrase themselves. You mustn't let people ramble on. Usually you have a good idea what they are going to say anyway."

The meetings of the Irish Georgian Society are, he says, very informal and "certainly not in any way pompous". He also attends meetings of the Irish Architectural Archive and of the Castletown Trust. "All these meetings are cultural organisations which are probably more loosely run than a directors' meeting of a fertiliser company or whatever which is probably attended by about ten men in grey suits."

Desmond says that chairing voluntary organisations requires tact. "A lot of people want to build empires and take over. Some people talk too much. They quarrel with people and make life more difficult. If it is a small organisation it is very unhelpful, but then that always happens with small organisations. Sometimes, there are people on a committee who have their own agenda and I do wish they were not on the committee. Frequently, voluntary organisations have the Irish problem of the split. It may be a universal problem, I honestly don't know. Division of labour is a very important thing if you are running an organisation. If someone is interested in what they are doing let them get on with it and don't interfere too much."

With regard to a chairman having authority, Desmond says "Well, I suppose you either have it or you haven't. It is quite a good thing if you have a certain steeliness behind the frivolity. You have to bring out the knives every now and then. That goes for all areas of life, otherwise you get walked on or somebody else takes over the organisation."

Desmond has never had to take a vote when he has been in the chair and he believes in consensus. If he saw a meeting moving towards a decision with which he was not in agreement he would terminate the meeting as soon as he possibly could. Afterwards he would talk to people and suggest to them another approach. "I think sometimes you have got to do a little bit of arm twisting before a meeting if there is something important coming up." He says he has never been faced with a complete impasse "This shouldn't really happen. These cultural organisations are not really in the same world as the financial world or banking where big issues are involved, mergers and so on. So we are really only on the nursery slopes. In small organisations like these one really should be able to get a consensus without getting into a major bind."

Desmond has no experience of going to business meetings. "No, I'm not a director of the board of Christies. The meetings I go to there are on selling, buying, and organising this, that and the other. People there play strange, psychological games. I used to chair meetings in the Victoria and Albert Museum about organising exhibitions and all that sort of thing in the years gone by. I found those rather intimidating. That was about twenty years ago. However, most of my colleagues were very civilised, very pleasant."

Desmond has observed many poor chairmen over the years. "They let people talk and talk and never pull anyone up by the straps. They let them yatter, yatter, yatter, rather like a fish on a rod, letting it reel away down the river. Never trying to pull anyone in. You've got to pull people in really. One of the most important things is

"A lot of people want to build empires and take over."

"They…never pull anyone up by the straps. They let them yatter, yatter, yatter, rather like a fish on a rod, letting it reel away down the river. Never trying to pull anyone in."

that meetings should not go on for more than an hour, I suspect."

While he quite enjoys being in the chair "it is not a role that I want to play that much. Lots of people are chairman of several organisations, but that's not my ambition". When he attends meetings he likes to see them chaired fairly briskly. If they are badly chaired he tends to drop out. "One eventually gets fed up and just doesn't go to them. There isn't the time to do everything in life. I think one tries to do too many things anyway and you should only involve yourself in things that really interest you very much. I'm interested in the conservation world and the academic world to do with art history and architectural preservation in this country and that is what I want to do. Other organisations I have been in for a long time and I quite often just fade out…"

Desmond Fitz-Gerald, the Knight of Glin, is President of the Irish Georgian Society; Chairman of the Irish Georgian Foundation; a trustee of the Castletown Foundation; a Director of the Irish Architectural Archive; a member of the Management Committee of the Great Gardens of Ireland Restoration Programme and a Patron of the Green Street Trust. He is a former Chairman of the Historic Irish Tourist Houses & Gardens Association (Irish Heritage Properties). Formerly Deputy Keeper of the Department of Furniture and Woodwork at the Victoria and Albert Museum in London, he is now Christie's representative in Ireland. Born in 1937 he is an Irish art historian who studied art history at Harvard Fogg Art Museum where he was a Teaching Fellow and received an MA in 1962. He lectures extensively both in Ireland and abroad. He is the 29th generation to have lived at Glin Castle where the family has owned the estate for nearly eight hundred years.

Chapter 7

Eithne Fitzgerald, TD

Eithne Fitzgerald well remembers the first time she was in the chair at a Dublin County Council meeting in 1982. She went to it well prepared and says she was not at all nervous. Chairing a group of this size with people from many political parties present is, of course, very different from chairing a small meeting of people sitting around a table.

Eithne thinks she is a good listener which she says is an important attribute in a chairperson. She tries to allot equal time to speakers and to pick up on things. "I have been to meetings where the chair doesn't listen and doesn't steer the meeting. This is like a series of advertisements where no collective view emerges. It is important to synthesise and to ensure that each stage of the process actually moves on."

Eithne spent a "big block of time" on the County Council, thirteen years in all, and she says the meetings were very formal. Having been around what she describes as the "meeting circuit" for a long time she has learned many useful tricks. One of these is always to watch the time and she tries to divide the time equally between people who want to speak. She says that preparation is the key to good chairmanship. Before an important or controversial meeting Eithne would speak to groups in advance. Her most difficult ever, she says, related to rezoning of land in Quarryvale in County Dublin. "It was hugely contentious and there were millions of pounds riding on it. I did a lot of work negotiating with the groups beforehand. And then I waited till the end of the meeting to say in what order I was taking the votes because if I had done this at the beginning there would have been an enormous row. I was determined that people would make unambiguous choices. So we started with the zero development option, moved to the 30,000 sq ft, 50,000 sq ft, and then the 100,000 sq ft option. So I very consciously waited till the end to say that we would do it in stages. Given that the meeting was so controversial it was very civilised."

Chairperson is Eithne's preferred style of address. "I remember the first time I chaired Dublin County Council in 1982. One of the officials kept referring to me as 'Madame in the Chair'. I felt like I was a brothel keeper. I prefer the style of chairperson."

When chairing Eithne says she is more of a mediator than a leader and she thinks it best to use the status and prestige of the chair to make important statements elsewhere. "What I have learned is that you are more successful exercising your leadership role outside at public functions with the prestige of office. At meetings you can bring people together, define what the issues are, move forward and summarise."

With meetings of seventy-eight county councillors from six political parties and often very contentious issues on the agenda, Eithne often met the different groups beforehand. "I would try to get agreement on time to be given to different items on the agenda, find out if there was broad agreement on an issue and perhaps get one speaker from each side of the house to deal with an item, rather than having something which was not contentious occupying four hours of speaking time because everybody wanted to make their 'me too' speech. Where there is consensus I think it is important to actually label it, to say 'these are the things we agree on'. Then what you do with that consensus is very important. Sometimes meetings are entirely taken up with matters where there is disagreement. The consensus needs to be followed up... I like things to be very practical. You can have a philosophical discussion but then you need to look at achievable targets. Let's have vision but within our vision let's take some steps today to do something rather than just letting things drift. Otherwise people go home and become frustrated because nothing has been achieved. Sometimes things can go around and around and people are reluctant to take decisions. Then the next meeting is the same meeting all over again."

When Eithne speaks of consensus she means reasonable consensus. She has experience of one person holding out against the views held by everybody else at the meeting and sometimes being very unreasonable. "If you have a multi item agenda and

*"One of the official
kept referring to me a
'Madame in the
Chair'. I felt like I was
a brothel keeper."*

34

"Where there is consensus I think it is important to actually label it, to say 'these are the things we agree on'."

one person wants to be heard on everything for their three minutes that person can really disrupt a meeting. I think it is important to distinguish between consensus and what you might call ultra democracy which allows any awkward person the right of veto so that everybody else is bending over backwards to bring the awkward customer along."

Eithne does not believe in precious time being taken up with routine agenda items such as minutes, matters arising and correspondence. At council meetings minutes are just noted. Correspondence, she says, can be taken at the end of a meeting. "The practice of taking these items at the beginning of a meeting has become routine so that when you come to the real business of the meeting everyone is asleep. I remember one particular constituency meeting where we had been asked in a letter to support something. People agreed generally with the idea but then we got to discussing the fine details. There was a twenty minute discussion on the issue. I wasn't in the chair but I said look, we are now discussing an agenda which has been sent to us rather than our own agenda. What are we doing…?"

For some people meetings become an end in themselves. "People enjoy going to meetings. They feel very busy when they are at meetings. And it stops them having to look at their desk which is full of stuff. They like the camaraderie of the meeting, of being with their friends. It is a social outing. And all of this takes over from what you are meant to be doing."

Eithne says that women are much more conscious of time than men. They like to get the business of the meeting done and then go home. "Women, by and large, have kids to pick up, dinners to cook, shopping to do. In my experience at union meetings men would go on all night until it was safe to go to the pub whereas the women would like to do the business in three-quarters of an hour and go home. I remember being at a meeting for local election candidates. The session was mixed, with many more men at it than women. It went on for hours, everyone repeated each other and enjoyed the sound of their own voices. The following evening there was a session for women election candidates. It was to the

35

point, people only spoke if they had something new to say, the meeting wasn't drowned in noise. It was all over in about half an hour. I think those present actually got something out of it. Women are much more interested in getting the business transacted efficiently and not coming back to relive the same meeting." An extremely experienced chairperson, Eithne warns of the dangers of being too directive while in that role as this can be counter productive. "There is, to some extent, a tension between getting your own priorities through and chairing a meeting. Your function in the chair is to get decisions out of the group. You have to recognise the validity of every member of the group and not ignore what the meeting is saying to you. If people feel they are not being heard, or are not having any effect on the final decision, this, I think, is very frustrating for the attender at the meeting. The meeting's decisions need to be clear, have clear directives and clear responsibilities. The chair can, however, set the agenda, and work out how much time to spend on different issues."

At Council meetings it is normal practice for people to speak in the order in which they put up their hand. When their turn comes the meeting may well have moved on to other issues. "This does not create a cohesive meeting. What the speaker is really trying to do is to catch the attention of the press at the back of the room. They are not actually achieving anything, and the County Council staff who are meant to be taking all this on board just sit and doze. They are not taking any direction from the meeting."

Eithne thinks that women are very conscientious in the chair and are good listeners. "If you go into a meeting thinking chairing is just about sitting on a chair the meeting can go all over the place."

Eithne Fitzgerald is Minister of State at the Department of Finance and the Office of the Tánaiste. Her responsibilities include the National Plan and legislation on Ethics in Public Office and on Freedom of Information. She served on Dublin County Council from 1979 to 1992 and was its Chairperson in 1992. She is also a former Chairperson of the Labour Women's Council.

Chapter

Frances Fitzgerald, CD

FRANCES FITZGERALD has been chairing meetings for so long that the first one has slipped from her memory. She well remembers, however, being at many very inefficiently run meetings where much time was wasted and people's talents were not used.

She sees herself as a fairly strict and targeted chairwoman, but she gets feedback that she is, in fact, sometimes too easygoing. "I think I probably have a sort of medium style of chairing where I certainly don't push things through. I really believe in allowing discussion. I like to get at people's real feelings about issues."

She readily says she likes being in the chair. "I enjoy it very much. I like to see decisions being taken and I like having the ability to move a meeting from point A to Z, to take people through the process of thinking out what is the best decision. I am interested in creating a climate where good decisions are taken. I get a lot of satisfaction from this."

Working on 'Women and Leadership' with American colleague Nancy Klein has, she believes, given her the ability to judge very quickly the quality of a meeting. Is the thinking creative or is the meeting merely ritualistic? "When I am in the chair I aim to create an environment which is a positive thinking environment which means that people believe they are listened to, that their views are taken seriously, that each one of them will have time to make their contribution. You need to have an environment which is more positive than critical. People don't respond to criticism. They respond to positive praise." She admits, though, that this can be carried too far.

Frances is in favour of getting decisions, if possible by consensus, but is not afraid to take a vote where she feels it is necessary. "One of the things I've learned is that one should not be afraid of going for a vote and I think maybe women don't use it enough." She agrees that this may well be because they are afraid the vote will go in what they see as the wrong way. Frances thinks it a

good idea for women to get practice in taking votes in smaller groups.

Apart from chairing a variety of committees, Frances also sits on a number of boards. These are not always run in a way she approves of. She particularly dislikes being asked to agree to decisions which have not been adequately discussed. "I have experience of meetings where I go in and things are given to me to rubber stamp as a member. I'm thinking of one board in particular. It's a rubber stamping exercise and everybody kind of colludes with that, goes along with it, because nobody really wants to put the energy into the items under discussion. Or they don't have the time to wade through documents. I wouldn't chair that kind of meeting myself."

Time is one factor she uses in exercising control at a meeting. She puts limits on people talking. If a point has been covered she will not allow other people to go over the same ground again. "I think there is room for tougher chairing in this country. Really, there are people who should not be allowed to ramble on the way they do. The chairperson must intervene and say 'we've heard this before'. People's time is precious and they deserve a quality meeting."

Frances strongly believes that tough issues should be faced into at the beginning of the meeting rather than the routine minutes, matters arising, report of other meetings etc. "I've used this tactic of taking the strategic issues first and it works well. Energy is high at the beginning of a meeting, so you tap into this energy and you take the ritualistic items later."

Women bring special skills to the job of chairing, Frances believes, and are often more creative than men. She sees chairing a meeting as a form of teamwork. "Women are not caught up in a macho performance, they bring a subtle informality and have more flexibility." She says that at times women are too timid but then so, too, are men. "I was at a meeting last night chaired by a man who simply could not control the meeting. He let people ramble on and didn't intervene. There is a lot of very incompetent chairing around."

For Frances, the worst chairperson is someone who will not tap into the skills, brains and ability of the people around the table.

"The worst thing is that they veer away from any critical discussion for fear that we might not be able to resolve a problem. They avoid the issue and try to force through a decision without any proper discussion."

Dealing with loquacious committee members is difficult, Frances says, but a chairperson should be strict. Sometimes she will not let a person speak for a second time until everyone at the table has had an opportunity to speak once. On important issues she would look for everyone's view. "It's amazing how often people sit at a meeting and say nothing. They have plenty to say but they don't say it because the talker is monopolising the meeting. I like to get the views of every member."

Frances is quite prepared to tell a meeting what her views are on an issue at an early stage because she feels that chairing is about vision and leadership. She feels that many people do not have the time to come to the meeting well prepared so it helps if the chairperson puts something on the table. In that way the good chairperson helps the meeting to look at the issues and move on to what is the best corporate decision. There have been times, though, when it would have been better for the organisation if she had postponed taking a decision, something most people don't like doing. "A kind of intimidation exists. Because an item is on the agenda, we have to take a decision. As I get older I want to believe my instinctive feelings more and act on them. Chairing is not the ritual we have been told it is. It's not just about arriving at decisions. It's about taking good decisions in the right context."

Frances advises anyone starting out to get all the help they can in chairing their first meeting. They should train for the role, get advice from outside consultants if necessary. "Get all the information you can. Decide on the structure and length of the meeting, and consider some team building exercises. Preparation will help to get over nervousness."

Frances Fitzgerald is a member of Dáil Eireann. She was Chairwoman of the Council for the Status of Women from 1988 to 1992; Chairwoman Women and Work Committee, Second Commission on the Status of Women; Member Second Commission on the Status of Women; Chairwoman Women's Political Association 1987 to 1989; Vice-President European Women's Lobby 1992 to 1993. She was appointed Chair of the Health Promotion Advisory Council by the Minister for Health in April 1992. She is a Member of the National Economic and Social Forum.

Chapter 9

Dr Garret FitzGerald

THE FIRST MEETING which Dr FitzGerald remembers chairing was in 1959. It was the Council of the European Movement which Denis Corboy had reconstituted after it had lapsed since its original foundation in 1954. "When I arrived he asked me would I mind chairing the meeting because I was neutral. I wasn't yet in politics. I was a journalist and academic and the other people were the trade unions, management, farmers, Fianna Fáil and Fine Gael, and because I was apparently neutral he ask me to chair the meeting. I agreed and I found myself in the chair for four years."

"I had to learn from that. It was easy enough because everybody was of one mind. We were doing something about preparing Ireland for participating in Europe. I don't recall a great many details, just the consequences of it. At that time we published a newsletter and I had to read everything I could find on Europe, and then write the whole thing, which took many hours each month. I edited the newsletter for four years. That was a consequence of getting involved in chairing that first meeting."

When he was appointed Minister for Foreign Affairs, Dr FitzGerald called a meeting of all ambassadors and senior staff. This had never been done before. "It lasted three days. We went through a very full agenda. I enjoyed that. The drawing out of their ideas, trying out my own. Seeing which of them stood up, which the professionals could shoot down. I had a clear view of what should be done. They were waiting for a lead. Getting consensus to emerge from the interaction of a new minister and of professionals over three days was a thoroughly stimulating kind of meeting. The important thing was to establish a relationship in which they would feel free to argue, challenge, discuss and debate and not be inhibited by wondering what my view was."

The Minister and his staff had two years to prepare for the presidency of the EEC. "We used that time watching how other people did it. Indeed, apart from my own role, there were about a hundred civil servants from different departments who had to preside over one hundred and eighty committees. Courses were organised by the Institute of Public Administration because some of these civil servants had never actually chaired a meeting before, apart from departmental meetings. The preparation worked and resulted in a very successful presidency."

Dr FitzGerald was impressed by the quality of the work of the secretariat of the Council of Ministers. "I decided to draw on their expertise. How meetings were handled would be of crucial importance. What seems a minor matter, such as the order in which to take things on the agenda, could mean you got stuck on a subject and failed to make progress. Then there was the question of the order in which to call people to speak. Who was going to be constructive? Who would be difficult? Who could be sandwiched in between other people? It was essential to identify the divisive issues, where they would arise and how you could circumvent them and put pressure on people to get the result you wanted."

"In order to initiate a discussion, the normal method is a tour de table. There are two ways, of course, of going around a table, left or right, and sometimes by switching it you might get a more positive result emerging. It is quite complex and subtle and you need to be well briefed beforehand and have good advice. You must know your brief. You must know exactly what all the issues are; what everyone's position is; what their strengths and weaknesses are; where they have got a problem that you can help with; whether it is a problem that can be brushed to one side. You must know all of that first. And then you can begin to decide on tactics such as the order of calling on people and the kind of pressure to put on them, and how you can get a couple of countries to support you on an issue... all that is very complex, rather like a chess game."

Dr FitzGerald deliberately decided to introduce a note of informality to the meetings he chaired. "The Irish, and sometimes the British, are better than the continentals at informality. When I presided at meetings I took my coat off. In those days I wore braces,

"When I presided at meetings I took my coat off. In those days I wore braces, my trousers wouldn't stay up without them."

"Another method of breaking deadlock is 'confessions'..."

my trousers wouldn't stay up without them. (A problem overcome by increasing girth over the years. I don't need braces any longer.) I would take my shoes off. I am not very comfortable in shoes really and I would wander around in my shirt sleeves, braces and socks, and that created a kind of relaxed atmosphere. I felt we had the advantage of a natural informality which in some ways takes continentals aback. In some ways they like it and in some ways they are disconcerted by it. It can be a way of getting things done. They don't expect it. We had a very successful presidency which was in part due to the fact that there was a large number of issues to be tackled and therefore there was much more fun, but also there was a lot of pressure to get results."

Timing is everything, he says. "If you have a problem, you break a meeting. You go and talk to people individually and try to sort it out. Another method of breaking deadlock is 'confessions' as they are called. You break and say 'look, I will see everyone individually'. You ask them to come in and say privately to you what their real difficulty is and how far they can go. You have to judge when to break; when to have confessions; when to push an issue; when to isolate somebody; when not to isolate somebody. It is vague. It is complex. I found it fascinating. I found it much more interesting, because of the complex structure, than chairing any other meeting I ever did at home, at cabinet or anywhere else."

His enthusiasm is evident as he recalls these meetings, some of which were very large with up to a hundred and fifty people participating. "We also had restricted meetings, with only ministers and foreign secretaries, to try to get it down to a mere twenty or thirty people. One hundred and fifty people at a meeting can make it very difficult because then every damned adviser is trying to get his minister not to give in. You get nowhere. The technicians are always trying to hold on to their positions. You are better off without them. On the other hand, unless the ministers have technical advice, they can make mistakes."

Looking back on past meetings Dr FitzGerald did not remember anyone he felt was an outstanding chairman. When asked about Mrs Thatcher, he said that she was good. "We had a

European Council meeting in December 1986 and as I recall it she was fair and thoughtful."

Dr FitzGerald says he did not have any one style of chairmanship. It depended on the meeting and the issues. "In Europe there was a clear and structured situation where you could work out your tactics in advance, plan them out and get results accordingly. Cabinet meetings, for instance, would be quite different. I had different roles for different purposes – Northern Ireland, ideological issues, which were complicated. You couldn't proceed by leadership, by vote or attrition. Too much bloody attrition, I am afraid."

"With Northern Ireland in particular I had a clear view of what I wanted to do. I knew my colleagues would be unenthusiastic about my involving myself in the issue. In fact, initially when I proposed the New Ireland Forum and had not prepared the ground with them, they voted twelve to two against, and I had to get them to change the vote next day in order to get it going. I had a clear programme. I would certainly consult the Government throughout. I would get their views and take them into account, but I was not going to be deflected from trying to achieve a particular result. It was the cabinet's job to advise and consent, I suppose, or to query issues and raise issues, but not to form any policy. That was never said openly, but that was clear to everybody I think."

Chairing estimate debates called for a different approach again. "They are debates which involve issues that would be tricky for the Labour Party and for Fine Gael, but usually the problems were more with the Labour Party. Taking a vote on the estimates is not a very satisfactory system because each minister is concerned that his position will not be damaged. He will vote down a fellow minister easily. If that happens, the fellow minister will vote him down next time."

"Maybe there is a more effective method but we didn't find it easily. So you could have very long debates on estimates, mainly because in our case we had to cut all the time, or indeed raise taxes. We had a period when all of the decisions were negative. We

"With Northern Ireland in particular I had a clear view of what I wanted to do."

*"People were critical
of my chairmanship.
I don't think this
criticism is a
particularly valid
one."*

never had a chance to do anything positive, so that, far more than any other government in the history of the state in financial terms, we had more difficult decisions to take. It was very hard to get decisions, and I was reluctant to, you know, take the decisions over their heads and force something on them if that could be avoided."

"Now, maybe I should have been tougher, but I think the relationship within the cabinet, which is very important, would have deteriorated if I had tried to force things on ministers, and then they would have to go out and defend something that had been forced on them. It seemed to me wiser to take time over it in order to wear people down and get agreement eventually rather than to force issues. It was a matter of judgement, someone else might have handled it differently. A long discussion may well be better for the Government, although ministers will object to being there until two in the morning. But, if I had clamped down at eleven o'clock and said that we were going to cut things off here regardless, they would have objected even more."

"People were critical of my chairmanship. I don't think this criticism is a particularly valid one. In the first Government certainly it was said that I pressed my own view too much and spent too much time pursuing hobby horses and there could have been some truth in that because there are things I do have strong views on. It took a while to adjust to the idea that it had to be the Government's decision and not just what I wanted. In the second government I did not pursue my own hobby-horses particularly."

When speaking of the cuts which had to be made in the estimates, Dr FitzGerald says that he often wondered whether a cabinet of women would be more rational than a cabinet of men in this respect. "I think men have more to protect in the way of status and dignity. This macho business. They are more upset if they don't come out having won their point. I don't know. I am not saying women would be different, but I just wonder."

The ideological differences between Fine Gael and Labour were few in number but "some of them, like the National Development Corporation, kept on going. They went on and on and on. There was the memorandum for initial discussion, the memorandum to draft the bill, the draft of the bill, the committee stages of the bill. We seemed to be at it all the time. There were a couple of other issues of that kind, not many. On issues of that kind you couldn't force a vote and have Labour voted down. That only happened once at the end of the final budget. But up to that point in the autumn of 1986 we had avoided ever having a vote in which Labour was on one side and Fine Gael on the other."

Dr FitzGerald says that one of the problems of chairing a cabinet meeting is that each minister is wearing a departmental hat. "It's a fundamental problem which has no solution. It is not a criticism of the people involved at all. Ministers are appointed to departments. They should remain primarily members of Government concerned with Government, but they become very quickly departmental ministers pushing their department's position. If they do not do that the civil servants or the public will make them feel they have failed."

"I did it myself when I was in Foreign Affairs. I was concerned to protect that department. The trouble is that when you come to cabinet it is hard to think once again as a cabinet. Every cabinet everywhere has this problem. It is universal, which makes chairing a cabinet more difficult than any other type of meeting. And the other problem in cabinet is that, as Taoiseach, you have to keep your distance. You mustn't be closer to one person than to another. You have to be more aloof from people than your natural instincts would prompt. Otherwise, people will suspect you of plotting against them. There is a need to detach yourself, which would not be the case in other contexts."

In answer to the question 'do you go into a meeting with a clear view of what you want to get out of it?' Dr FitzGerald said "No. Sometimes. Yes. Sometimes yes. Sometimes no. Not in the sense of going to a meeting and saying 'this is what I want and I am going to get the damn thing through'. That might have been true on Northern Ireland but not in other areas. You would end up infuriating everybody. If you are obstinate and won't listen to reason you will lose your

"Every cabinet everywhere has this problem. It is universal, which makes chairing a cabinet more difficult than any other type of meeting."

authority as chairman very quickly. If you are over-opinionated and try to push your view regardless, you will lose authority."

Dr Garret FitzGerald is Director of the International Institute for Economic Development and of the Trade Development Institute. He was Taoiseach from March 1981 to June 1981 and again from December 1982 to March 1987. He was leader of Fine Gael from 1977 to 1987 and was a Vice President of the European Peoples' Party from 1979 to 1987. He was Co-Signatory of the Anglo-Irish Agreement in 1985. He was Minister for Foreign Affairs from 1973 to 1977, having been Fine Gael front bench spokesman on Education and on Finance between 1969 and 1973. Dr FitzGerald was a member of the New Ireland Forum, and a one time Chairman and President of the Irish Council of the European Movement and member of the International Executive Committee of the European Movement. He has been a member of the Royal Irish Academy since 1974, a member of the Atlantic Institute for International Relations and the Electoral Reform Society of Great Britain and Ireland. He was a college lecturer in the Department of Political Economy, UCD from 1959 to 1973, economic commentator for The Irish Times *and correspondent in Ireland of the BBC,* The Financial Times, The Economist *and other overseas publications. Among Dr FitzGerald's published works are* State Sponsored Bodies *(1959);* Planning in Ireland *(1969);* Towards a New Ireland *(1972);* Unequal Partners *(1979);* The Middle East and Trilateral Countries *(1981 – co-author) and* Estimates for Baronies of Minimum Level of Irish Speaking among Successive Decennial Cohorts 1771-1781 and 1861-1871 *(1984).*

Chapter 10

Phil Flynn

Although Phil Flynn plans to retire in a couple of years and says he has already started to prepare for this, he still works sixteen to eighteen hours a day and Saturday and Sunday. One of his ambitions when he retires is to breed a greyhound Derby winner, but in the meantime he spends a great deal of his time chairing meetings where he tries to be "unobtrusive". "I try to let the meeting flow, try to encourage participation and try to avoid the dominance of any one person. I try to keep the meeting relevant and on track. I work for common ground, consensus if that's feasible. My style is to try to summarise options."

There are, of course, all kinds of different meetings but there are things which are common to all of them. All meetings involve communication, all meetings are done by rule, all meetings have a chairman, otherwise it's not a meeting. The first thing I do at a meeting is to make sure that everyone knows what has to be attempted and how we are going to go about it. I like to get a good exchange of ideas. I try to encourage those who are a bit shy, to make them feel at ease and to make sure they have a chance to contribute."

"I want to keep the meeting focused at all times because otherwise people become frustrated, demotivated. People just switch off. On the question of participation I ask people 'how do you feel about this?' I clarify misunderstandings and correct mistakes. If something was said which was factually incorrect I wouldn't let it go. All the time keeping the meeting on the rails, rejecting irrelevancies."

Phil says that he can be tough if he has to be but that toughness will not get him very far. He lists other qualities which he thinks are important in a chairman such as fairness, being unobtrusive, being supportive. Impartiality is important but for him there are some meetings where he cannot be impartial; where he has to sell something, to deliver a hard message. "The purpose of virtually all meetings is to give information, gather information, to persuade or problem solve. The most difficult is the meeting to persuade because your job is to sell change or to sell something which people don't want to buy. In that situation you are really a team leader. You're advocating something. Clearly, then you're not impartial. I suppose in all situations, but particularly in this one, you are in control of the task, you are leading the group, you try to maintain the group. In other words, you are working all the time for harmonious relations and you're trying to motivate individuals."

Obviously, bringing bad news to a group is very difficult. Trying to get people to agree to change is also difficult. "It's very easy to encourage the *status quo*. It's more difficult to sell change and I suppose at the end of the day that's really what we are paid for." Very often he makes the group look at the alternatives to what he is suggesting. He lists the points for and against a proposition. "There may be occasions like this morning when we had a meeting on staff changes. We arrived at a particular situation and we were very close to finality. I was tempted to push it to a conclusion but I made a judgement – no, we'll come back to it next week. I felt that since sufficient ground had been gained there was no going back. But there is a little more to be done and I've asked people to think about it. It's conceivable that there is a better way but one which doesn't reopen the whole package. I think that by doing it the way I choose people will buy into it. They'll feel more part of it."

Frequently Phil summarises discussions, for two reasons. It is important, he says, to consolidate the ground which has been gained. It is also necessary to summarise in order to avoid misunderstandings which can so easily arise. Negotiation is, he says, a skill but it is also a discipline. "It is the discipline of preparation, the discipline and skill of interviewing, the discipline of proper case preparation. Yet, there are inter-personal skills also. If all your contact with members or employers is going to be contact of a short brutal encounter then you are not going to make progress, so you have to be able to relate to people. What I am trying to say is there are different types of meeting and your approach will change. There is no blueprint for chairing and this is

"The most difficult is the meeting to persuade because your job is to sell change…"

"...to sell change... I suppose at the end of the day that's really what we're paid for."

good because if your kind of chairing is artificial I don't think you will be successful. If you try to be somebody you're not that won't work. That's not to say you should continue with bad habits. If you're inclined to be a bully..."

Phil always asks himself if a particular meeting is really necessary and if he judges that it isn't he calls it off. "If I'm not satisfied that it has a purpose I cancel it because meetings can become an end in themselves. There are people who are always running off to meetings. Meetings, meetings, meetings. The problem with meetings which don't have a purpose is that you end up with participants who become very frustrated."

Having observed others in the chair Phil believes that many people simply do not have the capacity to listen. When he talks of listening he does not only mean keeping ears open.

"Listening is a skill. It's watching body language being fine-tuned, trying to understand what is being said and why it is being said. Listening is the rarest quality of all. People in the chair are usually so intent on getting through the agenda, or achieving the objective they have set themselves, that they just don't listen. It could be due to a lack of interest, it could be anything. There is just a complete absence of the skill. In our job of negotiation listening is critically important."

Very few people anywhere have ever negotiated on the release of a kidnap victim but this was Phil's task on two occasions. The first time was when Dr Herrema was taken captive. "It is different and yet it is the same. The first time with Dr Herrema was successful, very successful. The significant thing was that it was done in private. The second time the negotiations were conducted in the full glare of publicity and that wasn't successful. Twice we were close to a settlement but it came unstuck. To be honest, I don't think you can conduct that sort of negotiation in the glare of publicity. The stakes were high. It was risky (in the sense that you might get on the wrong side of people and find yourself floating face downwards). However, the interpersonal relationships, the exchanges and so on were not all that fundamentally different. You are really talking of trying to persuade someone. You are also, in a

53

sense, negotiating because you are trying to establish what will solve the problem. Establishing what will solve the problem may be easy enough but the feasibility of that is another question. You have to exercise judgement – to know if you are able to deliver. For example, once the State is involved it becomes more difficult. The State is not going to encourage any truck with kidnappers, at least not publicly. So you're back to trying to build a relationship with the kidnapper in circumstances where you don't have a whole lot to offer, so you're into dialogue, into discussing options, trying to understand where all of this is going to lead. Then it may be that you find there are other options. You're back into motivation and why it was done in the first place."

Phil often interviews people for jobs which involve negotiating on behalf of workers. He is very clear about the qualities he looks for in the candidate. "I look for commitment, people who are really interested. I look for common sense, average intelligence. I look for people who are at ease with themselves and who have a problem-solving capacity. Now, these are rare qualities. If we find people with them we can teach them the rest."

The trade union movement is, he believes, just as relevant as it was thirty years ago. However, it may not be perceived as such. "As long as society is structured as we know it there will always be a need for trade unions. I touched on the subject of change. Change is inevitable and we all have to try to adapt to it, adjust to it. And, particularly in the last few years, we've had to cope with the pace of change. If you talk about change you talk about consensus and you then relate that to the work situation. Trade unions are a unique means by which group needs can be presented in a coherent, unified way. Recently in France, where union membership has fallen to between 5% and 10%, three companies offered to pay the equivalent of union contributions so that they would have somebody to negotiate with. Our agenda has changed but our basic objective hasn't – bringing dignity to the workplace. And the development of the individual, training and retraining."

Phil says that chairmanship can be learned by practice. It is important for a chairman to know the

"There are people who are always running off to meetings. Meetings, meetings, meetings."

"Listening is the rarest quality of all."

rules of debate and procedure. "I used Lord Citrine's book *The ABC of Chairmanship* which was published originally in 1939 but is still in print. People tend to grow into the role they are given. I think the important thing is that the person in the chair has the responsibility and the skill. Like any area in life, some people are born with advantages over others. Some have heaven-sent personalities and are just born persuaders. Yes, it's an art and that's what makes some people better at it than others. It's like athletes. Nevertheless 99% of people are capable of effectively chairing."

While Phil says that he doesn't even give a thought nowadays to being in the chair, there are times he prefers to be a participant. "Sometimes, I prefer not to be in the chair because it sidelines me. It takes me out of the milieu where I want to be. On the other hand, sometimes it suits me fine because I get the last word." When he is a participant he observes how others chair and he hates waffle and any time wasting. He believes it is very important for a chairman to deal with bullying at a meeting. He recognises bullies immediately and keeps them under control. "With experience you get to the point where you can very quickly classify the different kinds of people at a meeting, those who talk too much, those who bully, those who are negative, those who never speak. Even if you haven't met them before, you can say to yourself 'there's my bully, there's my talkative one'. You just have to handle them."

Phil Flynn is President of the Irish Congress of Trade Unions. He is General Secretary of the Irish Municipal, Public and Civil Trade Union (IMPACT), the biggest public sector trade union in Ireland. He has been a trade union official since the early 1960s, first in England with NUPE and since 1967 with the Local Government and Public Services Union in Ireland – until the formation of IMPACT in 1991. He was Vice President of the Irish Congress of Trade Unions from 1991 to 1993 when he was elected President. He is a member of the Central Review Committee of the PNR, PESP and PEW – a central figure in the creation of the social partnership and consensus approach at national level since the late 1980s. Sometime member of the board of the National Economic and Social Council, the Irish Productivity Centre, and the Institute of Public Administration. He was born in Dundalk, Co. Louth in 1940.

Chapter 11

Alan Gillis

ALAN GILLIS chaired his first meeting in a prison. Along with about eighty other farmers, he was in Mountjoy in 1966. At the time he was Secretary of his local branch of the Irish Farmers' Association. He describes himself then as being rather wild with a big mop of hair. In prison he was made the spokesman for the group and he persuaded the warders to let them meet together to plan strategy.

Alan had become involved in farming politics when, having qualified as an engineer, he set out to farm on thirty acres. The local NFA (as it was then) organiser immediately called on him and urged him to join them. "'I am only farming a wet week and don't know anything about it yet, and I'm not going to be much benefit to the NFA at this point.' 'No, but the NFA will be a lot of benefit to you', was the reply. I was a newcomer, a complete idiot coming into farming from the outside, and they made me feel extremely welcome. So I got in straight away. I think if we are part of an industry, we should all work together for that industry. At the next AGM I was persuaded to take office. And, like anything else I have ever taken on, I put my heart and soul into it. At that time we held eight or nine meetings a year but I decided that we should meet monthly. One of the very important things I always thought about an organisation is that it should be kept in PMO, to use an engineering term. We should always have it in perfect mechanical order irrespective of whether we are using it at the moment or not. It might be stored away in the garage but when the time comes to switch it on the engine should run. We had to be absolutely up-to-date and conversant with what was happening at headquarters and in our county executive as well. We were making things work on the ground."

Alan stayed involved in the organisation and benefitted enormously from his membership of it. He found the support it gave him very useful. He felt then that he, in turn, could help others. "Without breaking yourself in half you could do tremendous things for them. I got a good lot out of it and it is only reasonable that you should give some of your time back."

Alan says that chairing the National Council of the IFA and its National Executive is tough. The Council meeting could have sixty people attending it and might have an eleven point agenda. The National Executive would consist of the team leaders and the honorary officers. "So this is a real hot shop outfit. These guys are experts. I believe in introducing a subject, then discussing it and then trying to get a decision. So there are three elements in it, introduction, discussion, decision. As simple as that. Everything you do should embrace those three elements. In a voluntary organisation you have to keep reminding yourself that nobody is getting paid. So I really have to make the most of the talents they have."

He believes in going into a meeting with a clear view of the way he would like it to go but says that it is best if other people articulate the chairman's ideas. "People will be expressing different views and you could say 'I want to come back to John Smith for a moment because I think John had a very good idea a moment ago – could you expand on it?' His idea would be not too far away from my own." If a meeting was going in a direction with which he was uneasy he would say this straight out "I am less than comfortable with this but I must tell you why I am uncomfortable". "There are always people in the hall who will want to rush forward. Having come to the edge of the precipice they want to take a giant leap. Then there will be other people there who will suggest that if the President is uncomfortable we should investigate the matter a bit further as there is so much at stake."

At some of the meetings of the National Council there are often very weighty issues to be discussed and important decisions to be made. "I want the best possible arrangement or deal that I can get for the people I am representing and I want them to work for it also. I am talking about a decision which might mean £300 million or £400 million to the industry. So you have to be very careful to try to get it right. Any leader presiding over such a meeting has to have a

"…in a voluntary organisation you have to keep reminding yourself that nobody is getting paid. So I really have to make the most of the talents they have."

"You must never take a decision in `ignorance...try to get all the information available."

very clear vision of where he is going. You must never take a decision in ignorance. You should try to get all the information available. If we hadn't yet made a decision, and, if the television cameras were outside, we would have to make a statement on how the IFA had positioned itself. I would say to them 'a number of things have emerged from this meeting today (and pinpoint one or two of them) but we need to go back to the Department of Agriculture or to the Government to elucidate some point.' You can't ever admit that you haven't all your thinking done because then you are some kind of an idiot and the one thing you have to do is to lead from the front."

He believes that authority comes with experience and experience is gained by mileage. "You just start at the bottom as Branch Chairman and then you move up to the next step. Mind you, every step is fraught with fear and dread lest one makes a complete idiot of oneself. I remember going in to chair one of my first County Executive meetings which are very well organised. I said to them 'now ladies and gentlemen, you have just elected me to be your chairman for the next three years and I recall something my late father said to me many years ago when I was a little fellow which was as follows. It would be far better to keep your mouth closed and be thought an idiot than to open it and remove all doubt. I am, however, about to jettison my father's good advice and try to chair this meeting and try to do my best to lead Co. Kildare.' I think you must take control of a meeting fairly early on. You have got to lead from the front. Sometimes, you have to be a bit tough. Now, that doesn't mean that you beat everybody over the head, but you are the boss. At every meeting you always have two or three people who want to hog everything. They will come in and impose their own views irrespective of what you try to do. Now, there will be a lady sitting down in the corner not saying anything. You have got to try to bring her in because her thoughts are just as important as anybody else's. On a few occasions, perhaps a dozen in a fairly long career of chairing meetings, I have said 'Listen lads. Hold on a second. We are either going to bring some semblance of order into this or else I am going to ring the bell and we will finish the meeting' or 'cool it now. We are here to get decisions and this kind of behaviour can't be tolerated'."

Alan says that chairing meetings is not a simple matter, particularly in a voluntary organisation. "In a professional organisation people would leave it if there was a lot of rowing. They wouldn't put up with it. I try to run even a branch meeting or an *ad hoc* meeting in exactly the same way as if we are discussing a £3 million investment in a commercial concern. You have to try to give people the responsibility for making a decision. And a chairman needs to be seen to be fair, otherwise you get all sorts of caucus groups starting up."

When Alan was elected President of the IFA he says there were many internal problems. He had run unsuccessfully for the office three years earlier. "There were two main factions but there were another twenty-two small ones. I probably had the worst mess ever in the IFA. Every time we opened the papers in the morning we were in more muck. A number of people felt that I became President by default because I was the only person who had been nominated correctly under the rules. Most people accepted the situation but there were about thirty to forty people who didn't and they wanted more elections. And the factions were going to work against me. So I got into my car at 6 am on a Monday morning with the General Secretary and by the following Sunday at 1 am I had covered our twenty-nine County Executives (Cork has three executives and Tipperary two). I said to them all 'lads, do you want to continue to blow this organisation up by behaving the way you are? I think the organisation is more valuable, a lot more precious than that and we should really reconsider where you are all going. I have been elected under the rules as President and I will go through fire and water, hell and brimstone, to lead you properly and well. I promise you that I will represent you well and if I fail, it won't be for the want of trying. But I need you. I could do a very easy and comfortable thing, hand back my badge and say that this organisation is ungovernable, and some people are intent on blowing it up and wrecking it. But I have put too

"At every meeting you will always have two or three people who want to hog everything. They will come in and impose their own views irrespective of what you try to do."

'Listen, lads, hold on a second. We are either going to bring some… order into this or else I am going to ring the bell and we will finish the meeting…'

much of myself into it and so have you. What I am saying is very simple and I am going to say it to everybody. At the moment you are all on a football pitch but you don't know where the hell the goalposts are. You are playing back into your own goal, you are playing out over the sidelines. There is not a damn one of you who knows where the goalposts are. Now, I am the only guy around here who can show you where the goalposts are. Right now, I am the only guy who can show you how to score goals. You have until the end of this week to make up your mind whether you are going to continue to blow the organisation up as you have been doing very successfully over the past six months. Or you can get in behind me. That means accepting discipline. I am not going to spit on anybody. I am going to work with you as I have always done. The election is over; there have been victors and vanquished. I want to put them all together because the organisation that we are working for is bigger than any of us. When we are all gone and forgotten I want this organisation here stronger and stronger'."

Alan says that the relationship between the chairman and the secretary in a voluntary organisation or between a chairman and a chief executive in a commercial organisation has to be very special. "I would go further. I would say that the success of the company, the growth of the company depends on a good working relationship. It must be professional. You mustn't get into each other's hair. A good chairman must remember that his role is to get board decisions. He comes to those decisions as a result of position papers that will be put forward by the staff, not only the chief executive but others as well."

Like many other chairmen, Alan does not like taking votes and does not often do so. "I try to get a consensus. But, if you are pressed, sometimes you have to take a vote. If someone calls for one, you have to give them a vote. But there are often twenty resolutions on an agenda and you can usually get these through. You don't have to split the whole place up with votes. I always make the point that we have a problem when we have a vote. Because again we have the victors and vanquished. And then somebody, usually me, has the job of trying to marry this anguish again."

Alan Gillis is a farmer and a Member of the European Parliament. He was President of the Irish Farmers Association (IFA) from 1990 to 1994; Senior Vice President of COPA (European Farmers Union) 1993 to 1994; Deputy President IFA 1984 to 1988; Board Member of ERAD (Eradication of Animal Diseases) 1988 to 1989; Chairman Leinster Milk Products 1978 to 1983 and Chairman IFA Animal Health Committee 1976 to 1984.

Chapter 12

Mary Harney, TD

WHILE SHE HAS CHAIRED many meetings down through the years, Mary Harney does not like being in the chair. "Even now I much prefer to be a speaker. I like to participate in the discussion. When you are the chairperson of a meeting you have to stay relatively quiet… you have to be neutral in so far as you can on issues. I'm a much better speaker than a chairperson. But, with experience, you can learn the tricks of the trade. There is a huge responsibility on a chairperson."

When she is in the chair, Mary likes to start meetings on time, tries to ensure that everyone participates, gets a consensus and sees that decisions are taken. "I'm a good person at making sure the agenda is gone through quickly. And that means I have to put a lot of thought into chairing, decide what is important and what I want to achieve out of the meeting. I start meetings punctually because if you are always five, ten or fifteen minutes late people start turning up five, ten or fifteen minutes late and then you begin to lose your authority. You always have to show that you are a professional."

Mary likes to have a clear agenda and "I like to keep things very tight". She puts time into preparing for a meeting and would talk to people in advance if there was anything controversial coming up. "I would rarely go to a meeting and not know what the mood was. I think that is the essence of being a good chairperson. If you know the mood, you can think out the issues for yourself, you know how long to let people speak, you can dictate the pace. I think if you come totally cold to a meeting it can be awkward."

Mary attends many meetings of the Progressive Democrats but does not actually chair many other meetings nowadays. Their Parliamentary Party meets every Tuesday morning. "I would always take Monday evening or early Tuesday morning to talk to key people. If there was something on the budget coming up I would talk to the finance spokesperson, something on the North I

"The personality of the chairperson is nearly as important as the issue to be decided."

would always talk to the chairperson to tease things out between us – what we should do and shouldn't do." Because she does not chair these meetings Mary feels she can have a big input and that is the way she likes it. She is accustomed to being at meetings where decisions are made "and where we fly through things pretty quickly".

Mary says that to be effective in the chair a person needs to be competent and confident in themselves. Confidence is very important. "The personality of the chairperson is nearly as important as the issue to be decided. A good chairperson instils confidence; people are aware that he is competent and knows what he is talking about. If you go to a meeting which is well chaired you never really notice the chairperson. You only really notice if he is a bad one and chaos breaks out or if a conflict situation arises. In that kind of situation, the chair needs to lead people along and to inspire them with confidence. And, in a difficult situation, a clever way to end a meeting is to pose questions and not answer them, leave things open and come away from a meeting leaving yourself with a lot of power. If you can't bring the opposing sides together you could say 'look, we are not going to resolve this today, there may be other issues we should look at and, with your permission, the committee and I will explore other avenues'."

Mary has witnessed very many meetings which have been badly chaired and where chaos has broken out. "Certain people just don't have what is required and they don't have the authority. They lack confidence, they are not assertive enough, perhaps they are just too nice. They are not tough enough and everything runs riot… everybody ends up disgruntled. There is a lot of very poor chairing around." Mary says that in certain areas of life chairmanship is not considered as seriously as it should be. The giving of the chair is frequently handed out as a token, possibly as a reward of some kind. And she says that this approach can lead to chaos.

In discussing leadership she gives as an example a Taoiseach leading a cabinet meeting. "A leader is different from a chairperson. People have to be led. That's the job of leaders. Obviously, the leader of the government has to lead the government. That does not mean that in everything his view has to dominate. But certainly on key issues, yes. I'm not sure it is a good idea having the leader in the chair. I think chairing a meeting is about the ordinary running of a meeting where everybody feels they can participate, where they feel their voice can be heard. And it is all over fairly quickly. It is a decision making process. I think being a leader of a party is about leading people around to your point of view."

In an impasse situation Mary says that judgement has to be used to see whether "it is a compromise scenario or whether you can hang in for the final decision you want". When she was Minister of State at the Department of the Environment she chaired many meetings with different groups on the coal ban. "Chaos almost broke out at many of them between the environmental lobby and the coal lobby. In such a situation you have to have a very firm view yourself of what you want to achieve. Otherwise you just end up being dragged all over the place and the meeting ends up in a very indecisive way with no decision taken or a half-baked compromise, which just won't work. It all depends on the issue really; is it a vital policy matter where you have to hold the line or is it something where a compromise may work... it's a matter of judgement."

Time can be an effective tool in difficult situations. It can be used to wear people down. "The unions are great at doing this and meetings can go on all night. People get tired and worn out in industrial disputes – battle-weary." Mary has chaired many lengthy meetings in her constituency, often with two groups who cannot be reconciled. A typical situation would be a dispute in an area where they are about to impose a halting site and residents are all up in arms. And the travellers are there to lobby for this halt. The two positions are irreconcilable; this kind of meeting is very difficult. You've got to decide do you go for a compromise formula or do you let the meeting end inconclusively. You must take time and let everybody have their say. Once you have consulted you are in a stronger position. There can be a lot of repetition but sometimes this is the lesser of two evils. On issues like

"Time can be an effective tool in difficult situations. It can be used to wear people down."

"...if you want to isolate someone who is being deliberately awkward...taking a vote is one way of shutting them up."

crime in the area, travellers, rezoning of land, you get big public meetings and then all hell breaks loose. Now, if the chairperson tries to curtail some of the hotheads they can bring many people with them even though they are being totally unreasonable. You have to let them have their say and then shut them up. And you have to be able to deal with emotion. You do this by allowing a certain amount of emotion to spill over."

With very quiet people at a meeting who never open their mouths, Mary asks herself is their contribution important enough to ask them their opinion or can they be left out. Clearly, in a large group it is not vital that everybody should have a say. "But if you feel there is some Machiavellian person sitting down there waiting to catch you out then it is necessary to say 'what do you think?' Even if they don't say very much, the fact that they have been asked puts them on the spot."

With regard to taking votes, Mary avoids taking them if possible. "A good chairperson is someone who tries to achieve as much as possible through consensus and doesn't divide an organisation by having a heavy-fisted approach. But if you want to isolate someone who is being deliberately awkward and you feel you have the rest of the meeting with you, taking a vote is one way of shutting them up. But the consequence of this is that they could feel aggrieved and come back at you later. You could keep putting options to them: 'would you reconsider, have you not heard the views of the majority?' And I think most people, unless they want to be difficult, will finally agree with the chairperson."

Mary believes that women are much better than men at chairing because they are more conscientious. But, she warns, the woman has to be competent because otherwise the men at the meeting will try to make her look stupid. "An average man might get away with chairing a meeting, an average woman will not. A woman will start from a position where men just don't believe women are as good as they are anyway. There is a prejudice against women and their competence and there will generally be a certain amount of resentment. Men will try to imply that because she is a woman she is not up to the job."

However, if the woman is competent she might find it easier in the chair than a man, particularly if there are a lot of men at the meeting. "A woman can find it easier to get her way by using what is known as female charm... because most men tend to defer a bit to a woman. Men don't like to be seen to fight with a woman."

Mary Harney is Leader of the Progressive Democrats. She is the first woman leader of a political party in the history of the Irish State. She was the first woman Auditor of the Historical Society in Trinity College and Ireland's youngest ever senator. A member of Dublin County Council from 1979 to 1991, she was first elected to Dáil Eireann in 1981. In 1985 the Fianna Fáil whip was removed after she voted for the Anglo-Irish Agreement. She then co-founded the Progressive Democrats with Des O'Malley in 1985 and became Minister for Environmental Protection in 1989. She was appointed Deputy Leader of the Progressive Democrats and Spokesperson on Justice, Equality and Law Reform in 1993, becoming Leader later in the same year.

Chapter 13

Mr Justice Ronan Keane

THE HONOURABLE MR JUSTICE RONAN KEANE chaired his first meeting when he was at school at Blackrock College. He took the chair of the debating society. At university he was chairman of the dramatic society and of the English literature society. Between 1986 and 1993 he was Chairman of the Law Reform Commission where he presided over a small working committee of five people.

After his schooling at Blackrock College he went to UCD where he took an honours BA degree in modern history in 1953. He then studied at Kings Inns and was called to the bar in 1954. He became a Senior Counsel in 1970 and served as Chairman of the Bar Council between 1974 and 1975. He was President of the Irish Association of Civil Liberties from 1977 to 1979 and in 1981 he was appointed to head the Tribunal of Inquiry into the Stardust Disaster.

Judge Keane says that the role of chairman depends greatly on the size of the body you are dealing with. "In the Law Reform Commission there were only five of us and, while I took the chair, it was very much a discussion between five people at the same kind of level and the role of the chairman was far less important than it would be in other areas. Really, one's only function is to keep things on the move and indicate when a topic appears to have been exhausted, because somebody has to say 'let's get on with it'." Equally in a collegiate court like the Court of Criminal Appeal, or if a High Court Judge is asked to sit in the Supreme Court, each judge has an equal vote and the presiding judge is there to move things along. However, in a large body or at a public meeting, there is a need to keep order. Obviously, this shouldn't be necessary among four or five judges or indeed among four or five Law Reform Commissioners.

Judge Keane says that at the Law Reform Commission the other Commissioners rightly expected the President to take initiatives and to bring matters before them in the same way as part-time directors in a company will

"…people are their own masters or mistresses and they can allow themselves to be manipulated or not as they think right."

look to the full-time people to bring forward issues for consideration. With regard to controlling a meeting and exercising authority, Judge Keane says it is a question of force of personality. "A judge when chairing a meeting is not in court where he can ultimately enforce control by putting people in gaol if necessary. By force of personality, I don't mean authoritarianism or bullying, because that can be absolutely counterproductive. It can also increase disorder at a meeting. No, it has to be firmness."

Judge Keane agreed that in order to be firm it is essential to be on top of one's subject, and he also thinks that courtesy is important. "Be both firm and courteous so that you have the majority of people at the meeting on your side. If the minority which is being troublesome and creating anarchy at the meeting sees that the chairman has a majority on his side, then the minority should subside eventually, but it is very important that the chairman does not alienate people at the meeting by his rudeness or his bullying."

Judge Keane goes into a meeting with the objective of getting the business on the agenda transacted. He may have firm views on a matter and wish for a certain decision "…but I am always quite prepared to listen to a discussion and to allow myself, if necessary, to be swayed by what I hear. Sometimes, though, you find the meeting is going over something which has already been decided at previous meetings and people who are unhappy with the decision are deliberately opening the matter up again. Then, I am very anxious to get on because life is too short…"

Judge Keane sees nothing wrong with managing meetings, briefing committee members in advance or trying to get their support for a certain line of action. "I did not do it myself in the Law Reform Commission because it would not have been at all appropriate. But some chairmen might feel that if they are to get the best result possible for a particular organisation, they might have to do a bit of lobbying in advance, and I think that is perfectly legitimate. After all, people are their own masters or mistresses and they can allow themselves to be manipulated or not as they think right. If the chairman has the good of the organisation at heart and if the meeting is properly conducted, then there is nothing wrong with his alerting people in advance. Committee members may indeed welcome this."

Like other chairmen, Judge Keane feels that it is best to achieve a consensus rather than to take a vote. "It is fair to say that in a body like the Law Reform Commission I would very rarely have taken a vote. In a collegiate court, such as the Court of Criminal Appeal, the court is not allowed to disclose the existence of the minority opinion. In the Supreme Court minority views are, of course, allowed, and each judge has an equal vote."

When asked the question 'what do you do when you find a meeting is going in a direction with which you are not in agreement?' Judge Keane replied "Well, I don't worry about it too much because that, after all, is the democratic process and you would want to be a terribly arrogant person to think that you are necessarily in the right and that the majority is in the wrong. It is important though that you convey to the meeting very clearly your point of view for what it is worth."

If a meeting is at a complete impasse, Judge Keane feels it is prudent to postpone taking a decision unless the matter is urgent. "There is often a lot to be said for simply going on to the next item on the agenda. If there is a really deep, unbridgeable gap between people it is often much better to leave it and to go away and think about it. That can often resolve the problem. If not, the matter may have to be put to a vote at the next meeting in order to get a decision."

Judge Keane believes in dealing fairly strongly with committee members who talk too much at meetings. He tackles the problem at the meeting itself rather than outside it. "Yes, I think people really have to be dealt with at the meeting itself. It would be fine if you could go to them discreetly and say 'look, you know you are talking too much' but they would just be incredulous at that suggestion, so it is much better to give a little more shock treatment. It is better to interrupt them and to say quite firmly to them 'look, you have been talking for an awfully long time on this and there are others who

Judge Keane believes in dealing fairly strongly with committee members who talk too much at meetings.

"Be both firm and courteous so that you have the majority of people at the meeting on your side."

want to express a view'. And if you have received this treatment yourself in the past, it does rather rock you back. It may be a little upsetting for the committee members but speaking to them outside the meeting never has quite the same effect."

Judge Keane does not try to draw out the quieter or silent members of a committee. While he was Chairman of the Bar Council there were many silent Council members and he wonders why they bothered to go forward for election in the first place. "There were people there who never said a word. They attended meetings month after month, year after year, and said nothing. I just used to wonder why on earth they had bothered to go forward for election. I suppose from time to time they heard a lot of interesting things being discussed. They must also have heard a lot of boring things. I remember another chairman while I was still on the Council who used to ask everybody who had not spoken for their view, but they usually had nothing to say. The reason they did not say anything was that they had nothing to say. This only confirmed my view that if people want to talk they will talk and if they don't want to talk they shouldn't be there in the first place."

The best way of getting a big attendance at Bar Council meetings is to have a professional complaint on the agenda, it seems. "They always used to say in the Bar Council, and I am sure it is the same in the Law Society, except that it is a far larger organisation, that the best way to ensure a big attendance is to have a professional complaint."

Minutes are a very important aspect of committee meetings. "The whole point of a meeting is to decide things and to report how decisions are arrived at and, if possible, why they were arrived at, and you need accurate and comprehensive minutes for that. Every member should keep his eye on the minutes and make sure they record accurately what was said. But the chairman has a special responsibility in this regard. At the Law Reform Commission the secretary gave me the minutes well in advance of the next meeting so that I could check them myself. In some organisations the minutes are read for the first time at the meeting and that is quite ridiculous. Minutes must be circulated in advance. If there is a dispute as to what actually transpired at the previous meeting you may just have to alter the minutes or delete the record in its entirety and make some fresh record but you can only do this after a discussion with committee members."

Judge Keane says that two to three hours is long enough for a meeting. "People get tired of each other after that length of time, and that suggests to me that you are better off having a meeting in the afternoon because there is something about the approach of lunch which makes people restless. This is just a psychological feeling I have that the lunch hour is something not to be trespassed upon unnecessarily." Judge Keane likes to start meetings on time. "Accidents can happen, but as a general rule the chairman must be there at the beginning. There is nothing worse than waiting for the chairman to turn up. After that, it is a question of waiting for a quorum."

As a very experienced chairman himself, Judge Keane feels that a poor chairman is one who talks too much and doesn't listen. "That combination is, I think, fatal. I am sure you know the kind of person I refer to, the person who talks far too much himself or herself and simply does not listen to what people are saying."

He regards a sense of humour as a great asset for a chairman. "I think this is terribly important and can defuse a situation. Without being flippant, a sense of humour can take the harm out of a difficult situation. Robin Day on the BBC TV programme *Question Time* was a great example. He was perfect – the quintessential chairman. He made sure everyone had their say... he managed to keep things bubbling along marvellously. Whenever things got vicious or unpleasant he was able to defuse the situation through his personality."

The Hon. Mr Justice Ronan Keane was appointed Judge of the High Court in 1979. He was President of the Law Reform Commission from 1987 to 1992; Chairman of the Bar Council in 1975 and appointed to head the Tribunal of Inquiry into the Stardust Disaster in 1981. He was President of the Irish Association of Civil Liberties from 1977 to 1979. Educated at Blackrock College and UCD, he was John Brooke Scholar at King's Inns; Barrister-at-Law (Lincoln's Inn). He was called to the Irish Bar in 1954 and practised as Junior Counsel in Dublin until called to the Inner Bar in 1970. His publications include The Law of Local Government in the Republic of Ireland; Equity and the Law of Trusts in the Republic of Ireland; Company Law in the Republic of Ireland; Walsh's Planning and Development Law *(2nd ed);* Irish Law in the Twentieth Century *(in progress).*

Chapter 14

The Lord Killanin

LORD KILLANIN became President of what has been described as 'the most exclusive club in the world' (The International Olympic Committee) in 1972. He had been President of the Olympic Council of Ireland between 1950 and 1973, was elected a member of the IOC in 1952 and served as Vice-President from 1968 to 1972.

As a young man he rowed, rode horses and boxed and it was through boxing that he became involved in the Olympic movement.

In his book *My Olympic Years*, Lord Killanin lists the other members of the committee at the time: one Head of State, three Princes, one Archduke, three Counts, five Peers, three Knights, a Pasha and a Rajah!

Lord Killanin's family comes from Spiddal in Co. Galway but he was born in London in 1914 where his father was serving in the British Army. He was educated at Eton, the Sorbonne and Magdalene College, Cambridge, where he took an MA in 1939. His first experience of chairmanship was at university where he became President of the Cambridge Footlights Dramatic Club. He describes himself as being "obviously an extrovert".

On leaving Cambridge he joined the London *Daily Express* and subsequently worked on the *Daily Mail*. In 1937 he was war correspondent in the Chinese/Japanese war. Later, back in Europe, he wrote a political column in the *Sunday Dispatch*. "That had a by-line. I always used the name Michael Killanin. From the first day they wanted me to write a gossip column. They thought that anyone who has a title must know the social scene. I didn't move in those circles and I am a bit pink. Anyway, I wouldn't do it."

His experience of chairmanship can only be described as 'vast'. His biographical notes stretch to five pages which he describes as "very vulgar". This lists fifteen companies of which he either is, or was, a director or chairman. They include Syntex, Chubb Ireland, Fitzwilton, Ulster Investment Bank and

Irish Shell. He has been a member of the Cultural Relations Committee, the National Monuments Advisory Council, the Irish Red Cross Society and Chairman of the Government Commission on the Thoroughbred Horse Breeding Industry. He is currently Chairman of the National Heritage Council.

"I think a chairman is a sort of conductor. You have to know the score. I think there is a tremendous difference between chairing a business meeting, a charity meeting and a government commission. At a business meeting everyone is paid, everyone is professional, and they shouldn't be there if they don't know what they are talking about. Now, on the Heritage Council it is different. While they are all experts they are also volunteers, giving their services free. And one is a little diffident when they are all giving their time. Preparation is very important. Before a Heritage Council meeting, for example, I take a whole day to brief myself. These meetings last about five hours. Many people travel long distances for them. It is very important to delegate; therefore I am a great believer in sub-committees which report to the Council."

When chairing a business meeting Lord Killanin would be guided very largely by the Chief Executive and by the other members of the board. In the Olympic world, however, "I went to a meeting with my own ideas". He compares his style as President of the International Olympic Committee with that of his predecessor, Avery Brundage. "I think it is very important to make a few jokes and to keep the humour going. My predecessor used to pretend he was asleep half of the time. I smoked a pipe at all the meetings." He says that one way of exercising authority as chairman is to let people know that you know more than they do.

Lord Killanin gives the impression of being very relaxed, open and affable. He has a twinkle in his eye, wears half-moon glasses and now walks with the help of a stick. His elegant house in Ranelagh is piled high with books. There are dozens of pictures of him in his Olympic years at meetings with various heads of state. Decorations and awards from all over the world are everywhere.

He describes himself as a lucky person. "Shell was the first board that I sat on and it came about

"I think a chairman is a sort of conductor. You have to know the score."

78

"I think it is very important to make a few jokes and to keep the humour going. My predecessor used to pretend he was asleep half of the time."

absolutely by chance. I was in my club in London just after the war when a rather red-faced man came up to me and asked me what I was going to do. I said I was going home to live in Ireland. 'Would you like to be on the board of Irish Shell?' he asked. I hadn't an idea about the price of oil but I was put on the board. I eventually learned quite a lot. Some time later they were going to spend a large sum of money putting billboards up all over the country. I said that it would be far better if we had a good academic guidebook to Ireland. So the monies were switched from direct advertising to indirect public relations and I was given the job." In 1962 the famous *Shell Guide to Ireland* was published. "Professor Mike Duignan deserves a lot of the credit for this. His help was invaluable to me."

When Lord Killanin became President of the IOC two languages were used at meetings, French and English. As he is bilingual this posed no problem. "I used to listen in English but I would also listen to the French on my ear phones. Frequently I heard things mistranslated and this was very worrying. I think half of the problems in the world are due to mistranslations. It is very difficult to get expert interpreters. They really need to be specialists in the subject being discussed. Interpreters, like chairmen, must know what they are talking about."

During his eight years as President of the IOC Lord Killanin chaired sub-committees, the executive, congresses and sessions. About eight hundred people attended congresses and eight languages were used. "The Olympic Committee was dealing with sport but it was also very political. Politics featured very largely. Luckily I had been a newspaper man which is the best training for anything. I had also been a political press man and not a sports press man so I treated all sports equally, all countries equally. It is very important not to be prejudiced. You had to be conversant with the political situation. But this applies in business meetings also. You have to know the corridors of power. And on government commissions you have to work out what will be accepted and what won't be accepted."

In the Olympic world Lord Killanin studied the different characteristics of the various nationalities "because most people are, in fact, true to their national characteristics. You know who to flatter and who to attack. I treat an Italian and a German very differently."

Lord Killanin chaired some very tense meetings at the time the US and UK were putting pressure on the IOC not to go to Moscow for the Games in 1980 because of the USSR's invasion of Afghanistan. At a meeting in Montevideo he was determined to get unanimity on the Games going ahead in Moscow as had been voted on back in 1974. "It was a most difficult meeting, as were those with President Brezhnev and President Carter. It had to be a one hundred per cent unanimous decision and it was, although some people changed their minds later. I felt very strongly that we had a moral commitment to go to Moscow and I objected to the athletes being used by politicians for political purposes. And I objected very strongly to Mrs Thatcher's attitude. I think the only good thing that Mrs Thatcher has done is the Anglo-Irish Agreement." He left his UK colleagues, Lord Exeter and Lord Luke, to deal with her "and they dealt with her very firmly".

Lord Killanin flew to the United States by Concorde to see President Carter. "I came away from the meeting hoping that he was better briefed on international affairs than he was on sporting matters. Brezhnev was very well briefed. He had done his homework. One of the advantages of talking to Brezhnev was that you had a translator and this gave you time to think. Jimmy Carter thought he was speaking English but I couldn't understand him. I needed an interpreter for him too."

At times Lord Killanin goes into a meeting determined to push something through. On other occasions he tries to persuade, takes soundings and lobbies. He is always conscious of the people who are going to be affected by the decisions taken at meetings he chairs, be they athletes or factory workers. "I put people top of the tree."

Lord Killanin is Chairman of the National Heritage Council. He was born in 1914, was educated at Eton, the Sorbonne and Magdalene College, Cambridge. He began his career as a war correspondent and later became a political and diplomatic correspondent. He volunteered in 1938 and served through the war in the Queen's Westminster (King's Royal Rifle Corps), Brigade Major, 30th Armoured Brigade 1942-1945 and took part in the landing in Normandy for which he was made a Member of the Order of the British Empire (Military Division) and earned the Territorial Decoration and campaign stars. In 1952 he became involved in film-making with the late John Ford and subsequently produced many notable films himself. He was President of the International Olympic Committee from 1972 to 1980 when he was made Honorary Life President and awarded the Olympic Order (Gold). Lord Killanin has held numerous Government appointments including Chairman of the Government Commission on the Thoroughbred Horse Breeding Industry. He was a founder member of An Taisce – the National Trust for Ireland and Chairman of the Dublin Theatre Festival from 1958 to 1970. He has been the recipient of many honours and awards and was one of the first honorary life members of the Royal Dublin Society on its 250th anniversary in 1981. He is a Fellow of the Irish Management Institute and has been a board member of and has chaired many companies including Bovril (Ireland) Ltd; Chubb (Ireland) Ltd; Fitzwilton Ltd; Lombard and Ulster Banking Ireland Ltd; Northern Telecom (Ireland) Ltd and Ulster Investment Bank Ltd. He is currently a Director of Syntex (Ireland) Ltd.

Chapter 15

Craig McKinney

CRAIG MCKINNEY well remembers the first AGM of Woodchester which he chaired in 1982. "We had organised a very large room and had set out seating for almost a hundred and fifty people. We had also made catering arrangements for the same number. In the event only three shareholders turned up! I though it was like giving a party, if you have a poor attendance it is a flop. I said this to Brian Davy of J. & E. Davy Stockbrokers who told me something then which turned out to be very wise: 'When you have an AGM and nobody turns up you are doing a good job. When you get a full house you're in trouble'."

For Craig an effective chairman is one who has a clear, strategic vision of what he is trying to achieve. "At the same time, you have to be a good listener. You also have to be very fair and open and be seen to be so. Sensitivity in a chairman is very important. Sensitivity gives you the feeling of the meeting. It gives you a feeling of the competence of the various arguments which are coming across. If you are too dominant you are not really chairing the meeting, you are giving a dissertation and other people are just listening and nodding their heads. They have no sense of participation or involvement. It is very important to avoid doing this. The good chairman will define what the overall goal is. If this is not done each director will be operating to a different agenda. We need to sing off the same hymn sheet so that people will subordinate their own particular interest in order to promote the common good of the organisation."

Craig believes that a chairman has to be both leader and arbitrator. People will come to a meeting with their own viewpoint and see things from their own perspective. "In that kind of situation you are arbitrating between different interest groups and how they impact on each other. You, as chairman, are trying to paint the bigger picture and show people that their input is really only one component in the overall."

Craig says that the ideal outcome is consensus. To achieve this the chairman must know the views of a particular interest group, department or individual. "Preparation before a meeting is all-important. A chairman can help to bring consensus by identifying in advance the issues which are likely to be troublesome. Taking these up with the individuals concerned can bring a better understanding of what you are trying to achieve. I would always regard taking a vote as a very poor way of dealing with an issue." However, what he describes as "begrudged consensus" will only lead to disharmony on the board and he repeats the importance of sensitivity in a chairman. "You want to achieve a satisfactory result but this needs to be done in a harmonious way. Each board member is an individual person and has to be treated as such. A chairman needs to be tactful."

Craig is both Chairman and Chief Executive of Woodchester but says that combining these roles has now become unfashionable. "The Cadbury Report came out against it. The number of public companies which still operate on that basis is quite small, only ourselves and Smurfit now. I think there are some situations where, perhaps for historical reasons, it is appropriate. Obviously the size of a business has a particular bearing on the matter. If it is a small or medium sized operation I think you can quite comfortably combine the two roles. In our case, I think it will only be a question of time before we formally split the roles."

Craig, in addition to chairing Woodchester, is also chairman of some voluntary committees. "Chairing voluntary organisations is the best training ground for actually chairing a business. You are dealing with people who are not within your employ – they receive no remuneration. Their career prospects are not involved and they are giving of their time voluntarily. On that basis they are far more vocal in putting forward their views. I think hunt committees are the best training ground for public company chairmen. I've learned more from hunt committees than I have from any other activity. You have a strong element of factions within these committees. People often support personalities rather than ideas so you need diplomacy and patience."

"When you have an AGM and nobody turns up you are doing a good job. When you get a full house you're in trouble."

84

"I would always regard taking a vote as a very poor way of dealing with an issue."

Craig is also chairman of The Medieval Trust in Dublin which brings together academics and business people. "For me this is a change from the business environment. It's challenging and I get a lot of fun and satisfaction out of it."

Some chairmen feel that if an item is on the agenda then they should take a decision at all costs. They feel they are being weak or a failure as a chairman if they don't. Not so Craig. "If there are issues which come out of the discussion which are unclear or require further clarification, and particularly where there are people with strong opposing views, then I would not regard it as unsatisfactory to defer a decision. I think making decisions purely for the sake of it is a very poor way to run a meeting."

If Craig feels a committee member is too loquacious he will pretend to look at his watch discreetly but in such a way that the offending person actually sees him doing it. "I also think a pained expression on your face can be helpful from time to time." With non-contributors or very silent people he would go out of his way to seek out their views. "At the end of the day it is up to the chairman to bring people out."

Serving with a poor chairman, who is indecisive, is worst of all he says. "A poor chairman is one who is prepared to be swung for no good reason, who will abandon his own view purely because someone is arguing a case in a strong way. I think a chairman has to make sure his view is expressed and then seek the views of others. If people disagree with what the chairman is putting forward I think he should be able to argue his corner but then at the same time have the grace to defer to a better proposal."

Craig returns to the question of leadership and having a clear strategic view on a matter. He says it is important for the chairman not just to boldly state a view on an issue, but to explain the thought process he has gone through. In this way people can get behind the thought process instead of just listening to a statement. A chairman has authority if he is held in respect by board members. "How you exercise authority, if you are not held in esteem, must I am sure be very difficult."

Craig McKinney is Chairman and Chief Executive of Woodchester Investments plc. He is a Director of Crédit Lyonnais Finans Danmark A/S; Crédit Lyonnais Leasing Europe, SA; Crédit Lyonnais Leasing International SA; Dublinia Ltd; Leasimpresa Spa; Lookers plc; SIL Commercial Finance Ltd; Shannon International Leasing and Financial Services Ltd; WIL Ltd; Woodchester Crédit Lyonnais Bank Ltd; Woodchester Crédit Lyonnais plc; Woodchester Insurance Brokers Ltd; Woodchester Investments plc; Woodchester Lease Management Services Ltd. Craig McKinney is also Chairman of The Medieval Trust, Master of South County Dublin Hunt and Vice-President of the All Ireland Polo Club.

Chapter 16

Sylvia Meehan

SYLVIA MEEHAN has been going to meetings, taking part in debates and chairing meetings since she was a student in UCD in the 1950s. She describes her style as participative. It is all second nature to her now, rather like driving a car. She took a BA degree in Legal and Political Science and later, in the mid-1960s, got a Higher Diploma in Education. In the meantime she married and had five children. Her husband died in 1969.

In public life one of her first jobs as chairperson was of the Dun Laoghaire branch of the Association of Secondary Teachers of Ireland. "To me at that time this was not a remarkable thing – I'm not too sure anyone else really wanted it – but I found other people were quite impressed with it as an event in my life." Back in the 1960s this probably was quite an achievement, but she is modest about it. She became a member of the Standing Committee of ASTI and also served as Chairperson of the Women's Committee of ICTU between 1975 and 1977. She was on the Council for the Status of Women in the mid-1970s, and became the Chief Executive Officer of the Employment Equality Agency in 1987, having served as a member of its Executive Committee for the previous ten years.

Sylvia says that to be an effective chairperson you need to be confident. And it is also important to have the confidence to adequately represent the board outside the organisation. "Board members like to feel their chairperson is in possession of what is called wisdom, judgement or just plain common sense. If the chair is lacking in confidence then this will spread around the table at a board meeting or around the hall at a public meeting and then, of course, this gives everybody a very uneasy feeling. Everybody is insecure."

Her recipe for a successful chairperson is to be well briefed on the subject in general, know the running order of the agenda, know who is going to be at the meeting and keep an eye on the time. "Board members can become very

"...some women... have never had the experience of exercising authority in a visible manner even though they do it constantly within the family in a more non-visible way."

irritated if they perceive that things are dragging on and no decisions are being reached. But the people who become annoyed and who will voice their irritation may well be the biggest time wasters themselves. So there is a skill in giving people time to make their point and not allowing the same people to speak over and over again. And this is really a matter of energy, good eyesight and good hearing."

"I always try not to be rude or sarcastic to committee members even if one of them is breaking the rules, because it doesn't pay off. It lowers the standard of the chair. But you must be firm. If one speaker attacks another, then, I think, the chairperson must intervene."

If a particular member never contributes but always remains silent, Sylvia would try to draw them out, outside the meeting. "You might find that they are particularly inhibited or shy. The skill then is to find some area they are particularly interested in and give them a task to do."

A poor chair, in her view, is one who lacks interest in the job, who hectors the committee members or who gives the impression that there is really nothing to be discussed but that he or she has to sit through a boring meeting. "Equally, of course, any departure from a fairly calm approach to life, any loss of temper or showing of emotion isn't appropriate for the chair." Sylvia believes that the day is gone when men are curious about women in the chair. She hopes she is right about this. She remembers one occasion though when a chairman made an extraordinarily flowery speech of welcome to her as a committee member. "This might have been intended to put me at my ease but, in fact, only highlighted the fact that I was an oddity. And it is very alarming to hear a man say that we are delighted to see Miss X here as a representative of women because, in fact, one isn't a representative of women at all."

Some women, she says, may be fearful of taking on the responsibility of being a chairperson because they lack experience. "I think some women, because of their training and socialisation, have never had the experience of exercising authority in a visible manner even though they do it constantly within the family in a more non-visible way." She knows of one woman who was not inclined to take a particular post because it entailed a certain amount of speaking in public. However, this person was advised by a friend who had vast experience of public life to go into the Dáil one day and "hear rows and rows of men speaking far from adequately and still surviving. She could hardly be worse than they are," her friend said. "I think women probably have a goal of perfection and are eternally self critical."

Being the only woman at a large committee meeting can show up a kind of group behaviour. "When specific items come up on the agenda men will assume that you will be interested in them because you are a woman. That is fine if you are and if they listen to your presentation and then contribute themselves. But very often their reaction will be 'that is marvellous, great, now we will move on to the really serious business of the meeting'."

Sylvia says that on the whole men do not try to patronise women who are in the chair because "they assume that if a woman is in the chair of some organisation she is probably an awful lot better than other people. She must have been better within her own sex and probably better than the men available. So I don't think they patronise though they may feel a bit aggrieved if they see the position as one of authority and they wanted it themselves They may be very quick then to make points about procedure and protocol."

Sylvia likes to be called 'Chairperson' as this is the technical term meaning the person in the chair. She says that people in various churches and trade unions increasingly use this form of address and are trained to do so within their organisations. "I have no particular objection to being called 'Chairwoman' but I think it is ridiculous to be called 'Chairman'."

Being both chair and chief executive at the same time is difficult in Sylvia's view and she does not recommend it. When she went to the Employment Equality Agency in 1977 she held both positions. "It was not a situation I chose and I would not advise it because even if the person concerned can do both

"If the chair is lacking in confidence then this will spread around the table at a board meeting…this gives everybody a very uneasy feeling. Everybody is insecure."

jobs they will not be perceived as doing so. It puts an extra strain on the chair. There are times when the executive, quite rightly, has to put forward a vigorous point of view on the running of an organisation. This can cause resentment if it is coming from the person who is also chairing. And as a chair you might have to be prepared to accept a recommendation which the board might make to the chief executive. I don't think it is an impossible thing for a person to do but I think it is quite difficult for the other people sitting around the table to be understanding enough to realise that there are two points in the duties. So, no, I don't recommend it."

If Sylvia saw a clash of opposing views emerging at a meeting she, as chairperson, would suggest a rephrasing of the motion under discussion or indeed might defer the matter to a later meeting. She would do this if the matter was very divisive and if the board agreed to a deferral in the best interests of the organisation. She would always point out to board members the likely consequences of the different courses of action open to them and says that this is one important role of a chair.

Above all, Sylvia says the worst thing a chair can do is be on the defensive. If you have made a mistake, apologise and move on. "The worst thing is to be defensive. In fact, being on the defensive in any area of public life is the way to disaster. You get into more and more knots and you end up with no clear view of what is happening."

Sylvia Meehan (née Shiel) is President of the European Commission Advisory Committee on Equal Opportunity in Member States. She was Chairwoman of the Employment Equality Agency from 1977 to 1987 and Chairwoman and Chief Executive from 1987 to 1993. She has served as Chairwoman of the ICTU Women's Committee; Executive Member of CSW; Chairwoman of the Dun Laoghaire branch and Executive Committee and Standing Committee member of ASTI. She worked formerly as a second level teacher and Vice-Principal of Cabinteely Community School in Co. Dublin. She was born in Dublin and educated at Loreto College, North Great Georges Street and UCD. She married Denis Meehan in 1954 and has three sons, two daughters, one grand-daughter. Her husband Denis died in 1969.

Chapter 17

Ellen Mongon

IN 1993 ELLEN CHAIRED HER FIRST MEETING of the St Brigid's Travellers Women's Group – Tuam. She loves being in the chair and likes to get decisions by the end of the meeting. She knows the women on her committee very well and therefore was not nervous about taking on the job. She is also a member of a travellers' support group in the town. "I got experience because of the support group and watching a real person doing the job. I learnt from watching and listening. We brought our group down from thirty people to ten. There were too many people shouting. We have a secretary but don't have a treasurer because we don't have any money. We are affiliated to the Western Women's Link and there are seventy-five groups in this. The women get the agenda when they arrive at the meeting and I say to them 'we have two hours for our meeting – we are all here because we are interested. We will cut the chatter. We will allow each person to say their piece'. Now, if we don't have anything pressing to discuss we wouldn't have a meeting for a few weeks because this would be a waste of time." The women's group has about fifty members ranging in age from fifteen to fifty years old. The purpose of the group is to give them an outlet and to build up their self esteem. Most of the women see their role in life as that of wife and mother. Many of them drop out of school very early, which is a big problem.

When Ellen was born in the Regional Hospital in Galway her parents were living in a tent at Athenry. When she was aged nine she and her elder sister and her parents moved to a caravan and became stationary travellers. Her parents made this decision because they wanted their girls to go to school. "This was very unusual. Both my parents are totally illiterate. They would have gone to school only for a couple of days just before their Holy Communion to learn the prayers. My mother wanted a better life for her children. Then, eleven years later, we got a house and this was the greatest thing that ever happened to me because then there was no fear about not remaining in the one place. Halting travellers have to move on after a while. So we went from one luxury to another, from a tent to a caravan and then to a house. I coped well at school and left after the mock Inter. I had a high standard of education." She describes herself as a tinker, a daughter of tinkers of the travelling community. She explains that it is only the settled community who refer to them as travellers. "I never heard that word used. It is the settled people who use it. We would call ourselves tinkers or mincears. Even if settled you are still a traveller."

Within the travellers the king of the clan is the person they look up to and disputes are settled by him. He would seek advice first, get his supporters together and give reasons for his decision before taking on another clan. Marrying outside of the clan is frowned upon and could lead to a fight. Amongst themselves they speak their own secret language.

Ellen sees herself as a democratic chairwoman. She thinks that a chair should definitely exercise authority and should also be a leader. "Those people put you in the chair, that's my argument. You should make it very clear to everyone how you intend to chair the meeting. In my group there are people there who have never been to a meeting before. So, in fairness to them, I tell them how a meeting functions." She goes into a meeting with a clear view of how she wants it to go and she likes something positive to come out of it. If she feels that someone is unhappy with a decision she would ask them to spell out how they feel. "Even if nine out of ten people agree on something the other person should have their say and I would ask them to tell us how they feel. If everyone seemed to be in agreement on an issue they might not feel confident enough to speak up. You have to be fair-minded. Everyone is entitled to a fair whip of the lash. If a meeting was really split down the middle on something we would analyse the whole thing. We cut it down into little chunks and discuss it. I would do my damnedest to really lay things out on the table and would ask them 'have you sussed this out in your mind?' I would ask them if we are breaking any principles by doing such and such. That's the important thing."

"In my group there are people there who have never been to a meeting before. So, in fairness to them, I tell them how a meeting functions."

"I would ask them if we are breaking any principles by doing such and such. That's the important thing."

Ellen enjoys the meetings of the Tuam Town Commissioners but was surprised that at the first few meetings a new member was continually interrupting. She is intensely interested in many of the issues discussed (such as urban renewal) which are very new to her. "I've never had the opportunity to discuss these things before so I'm not going to open my mouth and declare myself a fool when I have no knowledge of what's being discussed. I'll tell you how cute I am. At the first two meetings I sat back and listened to absolutely everything. It was a time for me to soak up. At the next meeting for the first half hour I said nothing. Then I found the breeze coming in my direction. I found I was relating to what they were saying. When it came to my turn I took a deep breath and said what I had to say."

Ellen was elected for four years. "Two settled friends and Martin who works at the European Centre for Travellers in Tuam encouraged me to go forward. I was always spouting on about our voice not being heard in the town and they said to me that this was my opportunity. I was democratically elected in Tuam and its environs but not anywhere else so I don't have a right to say 'I'll do this or that for ye'. But, if somebody approaches me with an idea I'll go and talk to them. I will not turn my behind to anyone. I will fight for travellers' issues but also the issues of the settled people. I represent the two communities. To the people of Tuam it's irrelevant that I'm a traveller but to the travelling community it's a huge bonus. Up to this it's always been some outsider representing us. We have never had one of our own representing us before."

Ellen Mongon is a Tuam Town Commissioner. She is a traveller and the first member of the travelling community to be elected to public office. Born in Galway in 1964, she left school at fourteen to become a childminder and housekeeper. She subsequently studied and achieved a Diploma in Montessori Teaching and is currently a teacher at a pre-school in Tuam. Active in youth clubs and women's groups, she is committed to encouraging education for travellers.

Chapter 10

Professor Kevin B. Nowlan

KEVIN B. NOWLAN believes quite simply that some people should not chair meetings at all. This is because they have not had the opportunity to watch an experienced performer at the job. "Some people seem to imagine that you can put anybody into the chair and just hope for the best. My advice to an inexperienced person who is considering going forward for the office of chairman is 'don't'. He should first observe an experienced person at the job and learn how it is done. A chairman must know about procedure. He should be aware of the well-established rules and practices under which a chairman should carry out his duties. These have been worked out over a long, long time. Parliamentary procedure has been adapted to the needs of lesser organisations. The chairman must be well acquainted with the constitution of the organisation. He must also have a fair knowledge of how to read a balance sheet. That is increasingly important. Even though a treasurer may be there to give a hand, issues are constantly arising where the chairman must have a knowledge of how the finances of the organisation work."

It is important that a chairman should get the business of the society or company done and, he says, this is sometimes forgotten. "If a chairman can't get the business done, no matter how kind or pleasant a person he may be, then he is not a good chairman. That is the basic quality he must have. Now, that said, to get the business done in an efficient and competent way the chairman must have certain attributes. He must be able to understand people and that, I think, involves a skill at listening to what people have to say. He must be able to bring together the different contributions, to summarise fairly what has been said, particularly in a controversial situation. And he must also, I think, leave the members of the board with the feeling that they have had ample opportunity to say what they wished to say and that they got a fair hearing."

Kevin believes that members of a committee will normally listen attentively to what a chairman says provided that he is competent. Therefore, he can be the arbitrator in a contentious situation. He can also control the pace of the discussion. Usually, a chairman will have a fair amount of experience in the organisation or in some similar body and he can therefore give the meeting the benefit of his accumulated wisdom. Leading the meeting is, he says, a subtle and complex aspect of the chairman's task. "I think it is pretty hopeless if you have a chairman who has no real idea of what he wants to achieve or what the organisation is supposed to be doing. He must have an ability to speak on matters in a competent fashion. I would be slow to say that leadership involves imposing his views on the meeting. That would be intolerable and in the end he will be a very bad chairman. At the same time it's useless to have a chairman who has no ideas. Clearly, he must have his own views. He can't be merely a milksop but he must be prepared to be receptive."

Another attribute which a chairman needs to have is detachment, in the sense of enforcing correctly and fairly the rules of debate. "Both sides must be adequately and properly heard and no one should be given an unfair advantage. That is the role of the speaker in Parliament. This doesn't mean that the speaker has not got political views. He would hardly be there if he hadn't views, but he must be detached in the same way as a judge must be detached. A judge may have his personal views on morality and other issues but he must give each side in a case a fair hearing. It is the same, I think, with a chairman. Naturally, he has views of his own. Otherwise, why would he be chairman of the organisation?"

If the meeting were going in a direction with which the chairman did not agree Kevin says that there is little he can do about it. "Now, if the discussion becomes irrelevant then clearly the chairman must intervene. But if you dislike the way in which people are arguing or you find that what they are saying is disagreeable from your point of view, you just have to grin and bear it… It becomes dangerously close to imposing one's view on a meeting to say that a chairman is entitled to

"My advice to an inexperienced person who is considering going forward for the office of chairman is 'don't'."

change the direction of a discussion merely on the grounds that he finds it uncomfortable or disagreeable."

In Kevin's view, discussions have to take place with fellow officers before a meeting if it is to run efficiently and smoothly. However, he distinguishes between discussions to brief himself and outright canvassing of people. "I suspect that a large number of people would hotly deny that they would ever do such a wrong thing as to talk to people in advance of a meeting. But one has to talk to people, prepare and be instructed. Now, these conversations inevitably take place and it would be a very bad chairman who would go into a meeting without being properly briefed. That's common sense. On the other hand, I would regard it as a very dubious practice to canvass and try and influence in an underhand way the attitude of members. I think that would be very unfair. One can have discussions but one must be very frank at the meeting in saying 'I have discussed this with A, B or C.' Underhand practices will only diminish respect for the chairman, but preparation is essential."

Kevin B. Nowlan is Professor Emeritus of Modern History in University College, Dublin. Born in Dublin in 1921, he studied at UCD, Peterhouse, Cambridge and the University of Marburg, Germany. He holds a PhD degree from Cambridge and is a member of the Royal Irish Academy and an Honorary Member of the Royal Institute of the Architects of Ireland. He is Vice-President of the Irish Georgian Society; Chairman of the Castletown Foundation and a member of the Committee of Management of The Alfred Beit Foundation. He is a past-President of An Taisce – The National Trust for Ireland. He holds the Grand Cross of the Order of Merit of the Federal Republic of Germany. He has written on many aspects of modern Irish history and contributes to radio and television on historical topics and environmental issues. In 1992 he was honoured by University College Dublin for a lifetime service to the environment. He is also an Honorary Member of the Irish Society of Archives.

Chapter 10

Dr Timothy J. O'Driscoll

TIMOTHY J. O'DRISCOLL has been chairing meetings for well over half a century. Consequently, he has enormous experience in this area and is regarded as being a very able chairman. Along with intelligence he says that balance and coolness are very important requirements in running a meeting. It is also important that he can be heard. "A chairman must have the ability to handle difficult situations. He must be thoroughly familiar with the agenda, he must brief himself on all the business which is likely to come up at the meeting. He should go through the agenda with the secretary and visualise the discussion which will emerge under each of the topics. A chairman should be clear in his mind what he wants to come out of the meeting. This involves a certain amount of leadership. You must carry the people with you. You must give the impression that you are listening to what is being said and if you are a good chairman you will lead the discussion in the direction of the results you want. I think a chairman would have to have a fairly clear idea of what he wants. Of course, you don't tell the meeting that."

In Tim's view it is not possible for a chairman to be detached "but he must appear to be detached. If there are contrary views at the meeting ultimately he has to take a position and I don't think he can take a decision entirely on the discussion which has taken place at the meeting. He must have had his own views and he must apply these views when it comes to the point of decision."

Tim's definition of consensus is an interesting one. "Technically, consensus means agreement. But actually it means no violent objection. People accept the situation and they don't object to the decision. At international meetings it's amazing how you can avoid votes by getting consensus. And you can always arrange for pointed questions to be asked."

Tim believes that a chairman often has to talk to people in advance of a meeting in order to get them to ventilate certain viewpoints. "If the chairman does this himself he may appear to be autocratic or dictatorial. Where elections are taking place at a meeting it is particularly important for the chairman to have done some 'pre-cooking'. When a chairman or chief executive is standing down there is an obligation on him to look for his successor and to get agreement on this."

Tim recalls one meeting he attended which lasted three weeks. "It was a big international meeting in Rome but before that there was a meeting at governmental level and the real argument was whether South Africa should be excluded from the meeting. All the Eastern countries and the African countries lined up. The person chairing this meeting was an Italian minister who was utterly indecisive, utterly afraid that he would be linked to the West. So, we spent three weeks at a meeting which should have taken four days."

He also spoke of a meeting which, on the other hand, lasted only a few minutes. "Sean Lemass told me of a meeting he went to when he was retired. It was about the profits of James North and the Stephenson brothers. He arrived at it five minutes late and was astounded to find that the meeting was already over. So, the length of meetings can vary. I once spent seven weeks in Chicago at a meeting planning an international convention but it took all of that time." AGMs are, he says, usually a formality with the routine agenda items of adopting the report of the directors, the appointment of the auditors and the passing of the odd resolution. "Ninety-nine times out of a hundred they are entirely formal but there is the one per cent chance that the meeting will be contentious when, for example, someone is looking for election to the board. I always get the feeling that these people are unlikely to have much support behind them and, in that case, it is easy to knock them down. At an AGM if you haven't had notice of a motion you can't pass it. You have to postpone it and have a proxy vote on it, a vote based on the number of shares held. This is always an easy way to postpone a decision which might go against you on a show of hands."

Tim is interested in the idea of the chief executive also being the chairman but he personally believes

"Technically, consensus means agreement. But actually it means no violent objection."

102

"Sean Lemass told me of a meeting he went to… He arrived at it five minutes late and was astounded to find that the meeting was already over."

that the two roles should be separate. "The chairman is not in on the day-to-day running of the organisation. He can look at something in a very independent, objective way. He is detached. The first time I came across the two roles being merged was when Tod Andrews was in CIE. He was executive chairman and then there was a general manager. Now, where the functions of one began and where they ended was very difficult to determine. No, I don't see how the chief executive can also be the chairman and run a satisfactory organisation. If he puts up a proposition as chief executive he must support it as chairman. If he supports it as chairman, he must carry the board with him… There is the possibility of differences of opinion on the board which are very necessary at times. You have directors from outside so that they can bring their own experience to the meeting, add something. I think an organisation needs somebody in the chair who is entirely withdrawn in the sense of being outside the operation in which the chief executive is very immersed."

Tim sees himself as more effective in the role of chairman than as a committee member. "I don't know how many other people feel as I do but I feel I am a better chairman. I think it is the attraction of power and influence." At committee meetings he expects people only to speak when they have a positive contribution to make to the discussion. "The committee member who speaks because he feels he has to and to put his name on the record isn't much good to you as chairman… It is important though that you don't show personal dislikes of people in a discussion because that's fatal. People will rally to the support of that person."

He is attentive to the accuracy of minutes and checks the draft before it is sent out. "This is important because the impressions which individuals get at meetings can vary greatly. Even a very good secretary can produce what appears to be an appalling misstatement." It can often be difficult to deal with a committee member who queries the accuracy of the minutes. "In the absence of a recording machine, you have to depend on people's memories. And if the chairman and the secretary who took the record are in agreement, then the member who is objecting has to give way.

He might want to put something on the record and in that case he puts it on the record of the current meeting and not by amending the minutes of the previous meeting."

"It is important... that you don't show personal dislikes of people in a discussion because that's fatal."

Tim has a simple way of dealing with people who talk too much at meetings. He just doesn't look in their direction and doesn't give them a chance to catch his eye. "That is the simplest way of closing them out. If they interrupt and are really objectionable they will not get the sympathy of others at the meeting, so you can be very firm with them and get away with it." If people talk across the meeting, he does not hesitate to ask them to address their remarks to the chair.

There is, he says, a vast difference between chairing a commercial board and a voluntary organisation and a different style is called for. "In one case you are making decisions about money, expenditure, investment and profits. In the other, you are trying to ensure the willing participation of the members, to retain their support for your organisation. Since it is a voluntary organisation you have no sanction over them as no one is being paid. You therefore have to allow a much greater latitude and freedom of speech. In a commercial organisation you could ask for a director's resignation, in which case he loses his fee."

Tim believes it is important for a chairman to create a cordial atmosphere at the beginning of the meeting. "Even when the speakers are opposed to each other you can't start off in an atmosphere of hostility. I also think it is very important not to be too serious as a chairman. You can make some light-hearted remark and keep people in good humour. If, for instance, you are introducing speakers, I think you should add something other than what is written down about them on the programme. Add something which lightens the atmosphere of the meeting. I cannot over-emphasise this need to keep the atmosphere light. Lightness, cordiality and never losing one's cool. Finally, a chairman should have an air of self confidence. This is very important. If you are not confident, the meeting will not be confident."

Dr Timothy J. O'Driscoll began his career as a civil servant, becoming Assistant Secretary of the Department of Foreign Affairs in 1950; first Chairman and Chief Executive of the Irish Export Promotion Board (CTT) 1951-1955; Irish Ambassador to the Netherlands 1955-1956; first Director General of the Irish Tourist Board 1956-1971; board member Irish International Airlines; Chairman Algemene Bank Nederland (Ireland) Ltd; Executive Director European Travel Commission 1971-1986; advisory board member Gulf Oil (Ireland) 1974-1983; board member Guinness Peat Aviation 1982-1985; Chairman Board of Trustees Edward de Bono Foundation from 1984. He has acted as a consultant on tourism in many countries including Iran, Bahamas, Jordan, India, United States; was Chairman of the European Travel Commission; the Tourism Committee of the OECD; the IUOTO Technical Commission on Travel Promotion and President of the International Union of Official Travel Organisations (IUOTO). Dr O'Driscoll has been President of ROSC – International Exhibition of Art; President Marketing Institute of Ireland; Chairman Dublin International Theatre Festival; President and Chairman An Taisce – The National Trust for Ireland; Chairman Cara Cheshire Home Founding Committee; Chairman of CERT. In 1963 Dublin University conferred on him the honorary degree of Doctor of Laws in recognition of his public service and he has been the recipient of many honours and awards from Ireland and abroad.

Chapter 20

Padraig O hUiginn

Padraig O hUiginn is regarded as being a very skilled and accomplished chairman but he is modest about this: "I'm not so sure I'm accomplished, but I suppose I must have some basic qualities of patience and tolerance which I think all Cork people in Dublin must have to be successful."

When he worked with the Council of Ministers in Brussels he found that different nationalities tended to have different approaches to meetings. "The French, for example, will always start by arguing the principles before they get to the practicalities. If an issue comes up, the British, along with the Irish and Germans, would tackle it on the question of its practicality; what are the implications, financial or otherwise. The French, on the other hand, will start to analyse in a Cartesian way the principles involved without any reference to the practicalities. They will come later in the discussion."

"That is a fundamental difference between chairing meetings at home and abroad. You have to have regard to national approaches, to their cast of mind. Going further afield, to the East, I had a lot of dealings with Indian delegates when I worked in the UN and I found they had a deeply philosophic mind. They put the most subtle interpretation on every proposal which came before them. They would see implications – and I would say correctly in many instances – which less profound and agile minds would not have noticed. I am not surprised that in the academic world Indians are, on the whole, great mathematicians because they have this extraordinary subtlety of mind."

Padraig's patience must have stood to him when dealing with the complex characters of different nationalities. "Patience is, of course, the ultimate characteristic which all chairmen must have if they wish to have a successful meeting. The one thing which will destroy a meeting is having an impatient chairman who will not let people have sufficient time and space to state their view and who then tries to rush the meeting to some agreement. So, if people have a legitimate case to make, even if they are longwinded, you must allow them the time and have the patience to let them argue their case. You can help them by suggesting to them that what they really want is such and such. You can make a proposal. In this way you have helped them to make their point and shortened their exposition which by then is probably beginning to annoy other people. All of this is, of course, grounded on the fact that the speaker has a valid point to make and is not introducing red herrings."

Padraig says that a chairman should not go to a meeting with a prefixed agenda of his own as this can lead to problems. "But, if you have a fixed idea in mind, you must let the meeting develop to see whether your beliefs, your objective, your agenda are sensible or not. You must let everyone speak. Now if, in practice, you find a large number of people are of a different view, then you cannot compromise your position as chairperson by openly and aggressively trying to lead the meeting towards a solution which you think is best. You will never be successful subsequently as a chairman of that committee if you end up trying to force on the meeting a decision with which the majority of people don't agree. You can point out that the course of action they are contemplating has certain risks or shortcomings attached to it and might result in x, y or z. In this way you have served your function as chairman by bringing your knowledge to the table. In my view, that is as far as a chairman can go who wants to remain as a chairman who can function with the support and confidence of everybody."

Many people who chair meetings dread the thought of having a complete impasse situation. Padraig says that the best way of dealing with this is quite simply to put the cards on the table and say "We are divided on this issue, this is unfortunate. We shall have to reflect on the situation and have another meeting because the question which will arise ultimately is 'is it worse to do A or B or have a situation where we can do neither because nobody will agree?' In that situation it is far better to postpone a decision on that issue and transact other business at the meeting."

"I am not surprised that in the academic world Indians are, on the whole, great mathematicians because they have this extraordinary subtlety of mind."

"The worst possible thing for a chairman to do is to take votes. The whole purpose of a skilled chairman is to bring about consensus."

Padraig would not resort to a vote in an impasse because he says this can sow the seeds of later discontent. "The worst possible thing for a chairman to do is to take votes. The whole purpose of a skilled chairman is to bring about consensus. You may have to take a vote on the appointment of somebody, say between the candidacy of two people. Here a vote is legitimate. But to take a vote on a major policy issue is very unwise. People will attach themselves to one side. They will hope that what was decided on against their wishes will ultimately prove to have been the wrong decision and this will split the organisation. No organisation can survive a chairman who forces them to take votes on contentious issues."

It is better, he says, to play for time, to kick for touch, to come back to another meeting later on. These tactics will yield results in most cases provided that there is basic good will and that the organisation is united in its objectives. "What you must not let happen is to allow the discussion to become acrimonious. You must work as a chairman to convince everybody that those who express opposite views genuinely hold them in the interests of the organisation and you must not let the belief grow that people are being obstructive."

Padraig referred to his period as chairman of the National Economic and Social Council when the economy was in a very bad state. He presided over meetings of the social partners who may seem to have competing objectives but in practice ultimately had clear and fundamental common objectives and common interests. "In 1986, when the public finances were in a very bad state, the fact is that the social partners were committed to seeing the economy improve. Now, they started out not being agreed on what would be the correct solution to the problem. If you take the employers and trade unions, it is in the interests of both that enterprises are competitive, are able to employ people and make profits. Therefore, the whole question of consensus turned on how you would achieve that. You can only have a successful organisation or a successful meeting if people have a common, agreed objective. If they are not united on that, no chairman will ever succeed in getting an agreement on policy. There is no point in being together at a meeting unless you have agreement on what you are hoping to achieve. The role of the chairman then is to bring about agreement on how to achieve it. As chairman of NESC over some nine years we never had, as far as I recall it, disagreement on, or a vote on, the strategy for development and we produced three such strategies which turned into the Programme for National Recovery, the Programme for Economic and Social Progress and the current Programme for Competitiveness and Jobs. The question was 'how do we achieve this?' Then we got on to issues such as wage policy, tax policy and so on. It is possible, through debate and discussion amongst intelligent people, motivated by the same fundamental objective, to reach agreement and that was proved on three occasions."

Padraig says that a chairman should not show irritation with the verbose or unintelligent. And he must not allow himself to become annoyed with remarks which are addressed either to him or to another member of the committee. "You must always be sympathetic with every viewpoint expressed and try to keep the temperature of the meeting cool, collected and calm." Like many others, he has witnessed poor chairmen and described them as "someone who will not allow people to speak at length when they need to do so. The bad chairman is one who will not allow people to express their views fully, who interrupts too frequently. He doesn't appear to be listening and, clearly, he has an agenda of his own. He becomes impatient with people who are expressing views different from his. It is essential that a chairman should direct his gaze at the person who is speaking and, if necessary, take notes on what he is saying."

Padraig says that he would never lobby members of a board or committee in advance of a meeting in order to get support for a particular proposal or line of action. "That is very dangerous. If you, as the chairman, seek to manage the meeting in advance by getting agreement on issues, you then run the risk of vitiating the whole proceedings and bringing your own objectivity into question. There may be people

"You can only have a successful organisation or a successful meeting if people have a common agreed objective."

"You must always be sympathetic with every viewpoint expressed and try to keep the temperature of the meeting cool, collected and calm."

who do not share the view you are propagating. The fundamental rule is to do things openly at the table. In the end, you get far better results than by trying to stage manage a meeting in advance, which is a very dangerous technique. I have always cautioned against this. The function of a committee or board is to do its business openly and in full confidence with each other and not to go behind each others backs and try to set up prearranged decisions. You are dealing with a democratic institution in a committee. You run fearsome risks as a chairman if you engage in an attempt to get a foregone conclusion because there are always people who will object to that."

The agenda for a meeting is an important item and needs consideration by the chairman with the secretary. On a properly run board the chairman would get agreement for the draft agenda at the beginning of the meeting. "I think it is fundamental to the democracy and to the success of a meeting that the agenda should be formally adopted. It should always be seen as a draft which the board should adopt. There should always be an item Any Other Business so that members of the committee are free to raise issues which they consider warrant discussion at that particular meeting. However, one should avoid having discussions on trivial matters."

At Bord Fáilte meetings, which convene monthly, Padraig says that the meeting must run as long as is necessary to dispose of the agenda and transact the statutory business of the board. "There are functions which have to be performed and I think you simply have to allow the time. Time must not become a constraint." In the case of Bord Fáilte they start their meetings at 10.30 am, have a working sandwich lunch and go on until early afternoon.

In Padraig's experience, senior politicians usually make good chairmen. He emphasises the word 'senior'. "I find that senior politicians, on the whole, are people who are capable of running meetings very effectively because politicians are people who tend to have a rapport with the personalities of people. Therefore, they can conduct meetings in a way in which their concern is to make sure that people feel their views have been heard in a democratic way."

Padraig O hUiginn is Chairman of Bord Fáilte. He was Secretary at the Department of the Taoiseach from 1982 to 1993. He has wide international experience at senior level in economic and social development with the United Nations in Geneva and New York and with the Council of Ministers of the EEC in Brussels from 1973 to 1979. He was Chairman of the National Economic and Social Council from 1984 to 1993 and Chairman of the Task Force on Tourism in 1993. He was chief negotiator, on behalf of the Government, of the PNR and the PESP and Chairman of the Central Review Committee under the PNR and PESP. He was also Chairman of the International Financial Services Centre Committee. He is a graduate of Edinburgh University in Economic and Social Development.

Chapter 21

Frank O'Kane

FRANK O'KANE adopts different styles for different meetings. He tries to keep the monthly board meetings as friendly as possible, while the large annual convention of his Irish League of Credit Unions is quite formal and procedurally very strict. Up to one thousand delegates attend these annual meetings. "At small meetings I try to ensure that we don't get too hung up on procedure because I've observed that some chairmen get into that pitfall. They allow themselves to be hogtied by procedural matters. Now, you have to have standing orders – rules to conduct the meeting – but when it gets to the point that you can't do business because of some technicality, I wouldn't be hidebound by a technicality. I believe it's more important to get the business done."

"Our annual conventions have quite an intimidating atmosphere. My sympathies at that meeting are with the delegates rather than with the board of directors and I make that very clear at the beginning of the meeting. The board of directors, who are accountable, have a year to prepare for the meeting. I take the view that for many of the delegates it is quite an ordeal to get up and make a point in front of a thousand people. I would give the benefit of the doubt to the representative on the floor. I find that approach helps because the movement gets the feeling that you are sympathetic, that you are one of them which, of course, I am because I'm a volunteer. I'm not paid for the work I do and next year I'll be back on the floor as one of them. So I think that they appreciate that it is not a 'them' and 'us' situation. We are all in this together. Procedurally, though, I'd have to be very strict because you can't allow a meeting of that size to get out of hand. You could be tripped up all over the place. I would sit at that meeting with Lord Citrine's book on chairmanship on the table beside me. You will have people there trying to bring emergency motions, people who will challenge the standing orders."

*"I try to intervene
as little as possible.
I don't believe I should
be jumping in all the
time expressing my
point of view."*

The monthly board meetings take place in Dublin at the weekend. At these Frank likes to create a friendly atmosphere but there is, nonetheless, a degree of formality and they adhere to a strict agenda.

He is addressed as either President or Chairman and if anyone calls him by his christian name, Frank will take them aside and explain what the correct procedure is. He has found that one agenda item, the 'closed session', has consistently taken up more time than expected. At this part of the meeting all the staff members, with the exception of the General Secretary, leave the room and staff, industrial relations and other private matters are discussed.

He says that he now gets on very well with the General Secretary although at the beginning of his term of office the relationship was not so easy. "Under our rules, technically I am the Chief Executive of the Irish League of Credit Unions which is quite ridiculous. I delegate the authority to the General Secretary so he is, in fact, the CE under another name. He runs the office but I am in constant touch with him through fax or on the phone. Initially I didn't get on as well as my predecessor did. The fact that my predecessor was a Cork man and the General Secretary is also from Cork meant that they were on the same wavelength. But now I find I get on well with him. It was a question of putting down markers. I had to let him know that I am the President of the movement. The buck stops with me. When I go to the big annual conference, if something disastrous has gone wrong, I'm the person who gets the flak, not him." Frank sees his role as being one of leadership. "The fact that I've been appointed to the chair is because some people thought I've got some leadership qualities and I do have to give a lead. At certain times issues will arise when you are expected to go public. You have to become the face of the movement. Sometimes you have to go public off the cuff, often without consulting other people."

Frank believes a chairman needs to demonstrate leadership ability, particularly when there is a major division on the board on an important issue. "I believe the chairman's role at that stage is to allow both sides to have a fair hearing. We are basically a democratic movement. I can honestly say that we have only had one meeting where there was a major difference of opinion. There was a lot of discussion. Ultimately, we took a vote on it and the view which I supported was carried by nine votes to seven – near enough but the people who disagreed felt that they had got a fair hearing and they accepted the decision. It was obvious that there was no consensus so we had to take a vote. We could have gone on discussing the matter for three hours but I think that anything that had to be said was said in the first half an hour."

There are sixteen directors including the president on the board and in a complete impasse situation Frank would have a casting vote. "On major policy issues I wouldn't like it to be that close. I would prefer to have a consensus or, at least, a bigger majority." If the meeting were going in a direction with which he was uneasy he would strongly express his point of view. Again, he sees this as giving leadership to the organisation but if he is too forceful his colleagues might take him to task. "I try to intervene as little as possible. I don't believe that I should be jumping in all the time expressing my point of view. But, if a meeting is going in a way to which I don't subscribe I would state my position clearly and forcibly. The chairman should have the chance to express his point of view and show leadership qualities. But, if I was overdoing it, I would be reminded by my colleagues 'look you are one director in sixteen. You are the same as the rest of us.' I am *primus inter pares.*"

On occasion he has found that he has been of the minority view. This does not bother him at all and he would make no apology for this. Normally, he goes into a meeting with a fair idea of the way it will go and of the decisions he would like to see coming out of it.

He sees the effective chairman as someone who is businesslike, who understands procedure and knows the business he is involved in. He needs to have patience (but not too much!) confidence in himself and a certain strength of character. He must be able to take hard decisions and show a willingness to take criticism. "I tend to be a bit quick tempered and I can be very

"…my colleagues would say 'you are one director in sixteen…you are the same as the rest of us.'"

116

"I tend to be a bit quick-tempered and I can be very sarcastic." sarcastic. I do have a problem at times and I have to bite my tongue. You need to be patient but if a chairman has too much patience meetings will over-run.

In my view, the single biggest cause of badly chaired meetings is when a chairman allows too much discussion on a topic."

There can be a huge discussion on something which is the hobby-horse of a couple of the directors. They have a fixation, some particular idea or theory and can bring it up even when this is not the matter under discussion. When it is a genuine agenda item and the discussion goes on, then it's more difficult to control and the chairman should exercise the guillotine. Some chairmen are a little too sensitive and they don't want to offend anyone by not allowing them to have their say. The directors don't thank you when a meeting goes on hours longer than it should. Nobody thanks you. I've been described by a couple of my fellow directors as 'The Ayatollah'. This is after the meeting, jokingly, but possibly there's a certain element of truth in this."

The Credit Union movement is currently going through a period of change with the members of the larger unions now demanding a complete package of financial services. The image of the Union being 'the poor man's bank' is disappearing and many people now see the Credit Union as an alternative to the banks. Frank insists that no-one will lose out because they will still do what they were set up to do back in 1959. "I would foresee that within five years some Credit Unions will have automatic teller machines and inter-transfer of funds between Credit Unions. They will be able to give bigger loans for longer periods of time which will give them the possibility of lending for things which currently they couldn't lend for because the repayment period was too short. If you can give loans for ten to fifteen years that would open up whole new vistas. Not every Credit Union would have to move at the same pace. There are small Credit Unions in the west of Ireland or down in Kerry which might provide a service of a certain type, a service which their members basically want. They may not go in for ATMs or mortgages but they will still remain relevant and do what their members want.

"At the World Council meeting in Cork recently some delegates were critical of Credit Unions in Canada and the USA because they were too big, too commercial, but I believe that if the Irish Credit Union is to survive it is going to have to go that way. Otherwise, it will be like the land banks in Ireland at the end of the nineteenth century and early twentieth century. There were nearly as many land banks in Ireland then as there are Credit Unions now and they disappeared because they didn't remain relevant. If the Credit Unions don't move, they will stagnate."

Frank says that, as a result of chairing meetings, he has become more tolerant of people. It has also made him more confident in himself in his dealings with people in other areas of his life. "I work in a big school in Derry which has 1700 boys in it and I am the teachers' representative on the Board of Governors. I discovered when I joined the board that my knowledge of meetings and procedure was a great help. The confidence which I had gained allowed me to become a much stronger person at those meetings and far more articulate."

Frank O'Kane is President of the Irish League of Credit Unions. A long-time director and former President of Pennyburn Credit Union, he is the third Derryman to be elected President of the League following John Hume in the 1960s and Eugene O'Brien in the early 1980s. Elected to the board in 1986, he has served since then on all of the League's committees and has been especially active in promoting credit union development in the poorer countries of the world, especially in Africa. He is a teacher at St Columb's College, Derry.

Chapter 22

Olivia O'Leary

OLIVIA O'LEARY believes that calmness and determination are two important qualities in a chairperson. You have to be quite determined, she says, but, of course "you mustn't lose your rag". Sometimes people at meetings are extraordinarily obdurate and therefore the chair also needs to be tough.

When chairing television discussions, it is the way she brings people out which is important rather than the conclusion. "It is important that I concentrate on the way I draw them out, on the way they speak, on the way the whole thing forms itself because, after all, I have time to fill and I am in the process of entertaining and informing as well as arriving at a conclusion. For me, it is important that it is lively. There are many business meetings where it would not particularly matter if one person spoke the whole time as long as a conclusion was reached. Now, that is no use to me… I need everybody to take part. This is a dance. This has a shape. And obviously, if you are going to chair it well, you will come into it with a clear view of what that shape will be, of what the structure will be and that everybody understands this, so that they can take part in the process. I would have to drive it towards some sort of conclusion so that the viewers feel we are getting somewhere. Whereas sometimes in business meetings it may tactically be a very useful thing to leave a discussion hanging in the air, I feel the need to push towards a conclusion so that it makes sense for the viewers. I would tend to summarise, to push people to give me a yes/no answer. I would tend to make them focus and make them declare their hand. Now, business meetings wouldn't always work that way."

She says that if consensus emerges, that is great, but that at times people pretend to agree to something which she knows they really don't. "My job as a journalist, if this doesn't sound too pompous, is to try to get at the truth. Both the truth about things which have happened and the truth of people's attitudes towards things which have happened. So it is my job to get at it no matter how

"If people are slow to say what they think, slow to put their argument forward, then you have to give them a kick-start."

it comes out. Sometimes in business meetings, it suits everybody to connive at what, in fact, is not the truth, at what is an untruth or a pretence. I would regard it as my job to keep on pushing until I get people to say what is their true position."

Olivia says that she would not try to create rifts on a programme, where they don't exist, in order to liven things up. "It isn't my job to start sowing seeds of dissent where none exists. Everybody would realise I am picking a row. But, in the nature of television programmes, we won't choose people who will all be of the one view. But where they are all trying to pretend that they are equally in favour of religion and the family and I know damn well from both their attitudes and their private lives that this is not the case, but it suits them politically to say so at a particular time, well then I will poke, by God, I'll poke."

Olivia believes in having people of opposing views on her programmes so that she can get elucidation through argument. "I think argument and dialectic help to elucidate. Margaret Thatcher always thought so. She thought that the best way to come to decisions was through forcing argument so that by hearing the toughest opposition to her own position she might learn. She learnt through argument. Now, I think there is a lot to be said for that. I also think that at all meetings, whether it is a television programme, a business meeting or a major policy conference, you do need a structure. Have a plan of how you are going to begin it, how you are going to conduct it and how you are going to end it. It must not be just an arbitrary thing. Sometimes your authority as chairperson depends on people knowing that you have a structure in mind which is going to include them all and that everybody is going to get a go. So, I feel that you must come into the meeting and explain at the beginning how it is going to operate. Then people will feel 'OK, she has got it under control, she knows what she is doing. I will wait my turn because I will get my say'. And therefore you establish a trust and authority with the people you are chairing."

Olivia says that sometimes a chairperson has to be both a leader and an arbiter. "One is an arbiter when there are two warring factions, two clearly opposed views, then you mediate. But, when your role is to draw people out, then you must lead. Particularly if people are slow to say what they think, slow to put their argument forward, then you have to give them a kick-start. You have to lead and you have to take an editorial decision to push a line of argument at them in order to get them to react."

Being consistent in the treatment of people helps to establish trust and respect. She has to guard against people exploiting their time at the microphone. "You try to discipline them and if you have to hurry them along you try to do it with humour. A lot of people talk about courtesy. I think courtesy is all very well, but in this day and age people exploit courtesy. I have to tone down what might seem like an abrupt interruption with a certain amount of humour. People can't be seen to object to humour."

Olivia describes her style as very much "hands-on". "That is the nature of my job. Unless things are bumbling along nicely, I believe in getting involved and pushing people along. They have to be kept on the path and hurried along."

She says that listening, watching and focusing attention are vitally important in a chairperson. "You have to listen with every bit of yourself to what is going on. And watch people, look at reactions, take in all the vibes. You must make connections between what people say. I usually let people confirm what they have said to make sure there is a clear view around the table because there is no point in having half-baked ideas of what has happened. I think you must take charge, you must drive to a conclusion because people get very impatient if they feel nobody is driving a meeting. They lose interest."

Olivia likens coping with an impasse situation to playing doubles in tennis. "You take the attitude or point of view of one group and put it to the other people, going from person to person and there will often be some sort of compromise, some *rapprochement*. At least you open a door for people to talk to one another. If they can't talk to one another on a policy level or on a political level, they will sometimes be able to talk to one another as individuals and they can bring things forward a little."

"I think courtesy is all very well, but in this day and age people exploit courtesy."

"You have to listen with every bit of yourself to what is going on."

In Olivia's view it is no more difficult for a woman nowadays to be an effective chairperson than it is for a man. "Men don't feel humiliated any more by the fact of there being a woman in the chair whereas before they felt the need to be difficult, obdurate and patronising. You will still get the odd one. But usually, when you pick him up and point out to him that you know exactly what he is doing, he will be a little taken aback. Political correctness has advanced to the stage where certain things are not acceptable any more. Even if men believe privately that women are second-class citizens they can't say it any more."

Olivia is quite tough with people who talk too much or who try to dominate the discussion. People at the meeting will be grateful to the chairperson if they step in to restrain the verbose speaker and the trick is simply not to give them the floor too often. "I would say to them 'now Jim, we know you like to put your point at length but this time, Jim, we do not want you to put your point at length'. Sometimes just to point out to them that they are long-winded will make them self-conscious. It also means that when they are getting into their third wind, you can interrupt them because, as they have been forewarned, you are not being unfair."

On television programmes she also has to watch for people who give monosyllabic answers. "They drop you in it. They answer 'no' to a question and you wait for them to go on but they don't. And that is where, if you are not listening, you can land in trouble. Particularly at the beginning of a programme there is a great temptation for me to sit back, check my notes, check where everybody is while a speaker is getting into his or her stride. So you have to be ready. That is where listening comes in. I can never assume that somebody is going to give a thirty second or a one minute answer. Usually you handle it by pressing them to elucidate the point. I think also when a chairperson has a problem, the best thing to do is to share it with other people rather than try to cover it over. It is much better if I turn around and say to whoever it is 'listen you are being very laconic this evening, is there any particular reason why? Would you like to share the full fruits of your great deliberations with us?' With a certain amount of humour you can get people to come out a little and now usually they will feel ashamed of being obdurate, or difficult. But I think it is a problem you share with everybody."

Olivia's first time in the chair was at a debate in her convent school, St. Leo's in Carlow. She also contributed to the debate "which wasn't the ideal position to be in. I was astounded to find out that the view which I held wasn't one that was held by everybody else. We were talking about music, country and western versus rock, and I assumed that everybody my age would be rock fans. But when the debate got going it was obvious from the audience that I was outnumbered by about four to one. It was a fairly humiliating experience."

She says that this experience taught her to get to know her audience or the participants in a discussion. She finds out what will agitate them. Before doing a programme Olivia spends a lot of time on the phone talking to a whole range of people to take soundings. "I talk to the most unlikely people. Very often I ring people who are quite far flung, people outside my world in here. This can be very useful because outside our little world I often find that there is not the same interest in a subject or the emphasis is very different from what we might have expected."

She recalls with amusement her worst ever television programme when two Cork men were at each other's throats. All her efforts to stop them from shouting at each other failed but she remained calm throughout. "They were talking so fast in Cork accents that it was very hard to understand anything they were saying. They were talking on top of one another all the time. For ten minutes I made various attempts to interject but in the end I realised it was pointless. It is the only time I ever remember people getting so locked into one another that they wouldn't allow the other person to speak for even three seconds. So the rule is never put two Cork men on together!"

Olivia says that a poor chair is one who does not listen. "People who don't listen and people who don't remember names. They don't remember what has been said and they don't drive to a conclusion. All of this drives me crazy."

Olivia O'Leary is a journalist. She worked as a reporter with the Nationalist and Leinster Times *from 1969 to 1972; with RTE from 1972 to 1978 and with* The Irish Times *from 1978 to 1984. She presented the BBC television programme* Newsnight *from 1985 to 1986 and RTE's* Today Tonight *and* Questions and Answers *from 1986 to 1988; she was also presenter of* First Tuesday *on Yorkshire TV. She received three Jacobs Awards for her work on radio (1974) and television (1982 and 1987).*

Chapter 23

Dr A.J.F. O'Reilly

"CHAIRMEN NEED TO BE CHARMING" says Tony O'Reilly. Dealing with verbose people needs patience and a chairman must not allow himself to show irritation. "We have what you might describe as people who suffer from a dose of the predictabilities. In other words, when they start to speak they will speak for ten minutes and they will repeat every *cliché* that has been spoken on the same topic for the last ten years with the same anecdotal evidence and you just have to endure that. Obviously, if they try to do the same thing twice in the same meeting you bring it to a close. And that is where wit, humour, style, grace and charm come in."

His most difficult meetings ever were in 1975 and 1976 when Fitzwilton was going through a very bad period. "We were battling against, essentially, being put out of business and the public meetings I chaired were very tough. Those were difficult times when the world fertiliser market collapsed. We had unusable plant in Dublin, a thousand people out of work and £19m. losses. We fought our way back but we had all those meetings I had to chair and they were horrendous. I mean horrendous. I was determined not to show any gross irritation. People who had waited a year to have a go at us got up and really shafted us. You have to understand that they saw a share which had been worth a hundred was now worth fifty. They had lost half of their money... so I understood this. They were asking questions and I knew I had to show equanimity, that I must be gracious and graceful. One of the shareholders, a lovely lawyer, had this line 'I consider the conduct of this meeting to be quite churlish. I personally consider it a great honour to have lost money with Dr O'Reilly'. It was a double-edged comment. I really thought it was the ultimate irony."

Tony describes his style of chairmanship as "attentive". He says a chairman at any meeting has to gauge the temper of the meeting by listening to the initial opening flourishes of everybody on a given topic. "If the subject is one in which there is a great deal of intensity well then, quite obviously, you will know the room will divide itself into antagonists and protagonists. So, in all of those sorts of meetings, and there are thousands of different meetings, the first rule is the rule of rugby football which is to be attentive to the opposition, to find out what they are going to do and then to decide upon your tactics, rather than to go in with a firm plan 'this is the way I am going to run this meeting'."

He says that a chairman needs to be a leader to be a good arbitrator. "At a meeting people need to feel they have had their day in court and that the scales of justice have been weighted fairly and evenly and that both points of view have been, if not reconciled, at least evaluated. It requires a hell of a lot of leadership to be able to say authoritatively 'look John, I think we have given you a fair day in court and Joe, we have listened to your contradictory views, but you know that the general sense of this meeting is that John's view must prevail and for the following eight reasons'..." He stressed that objectivity is an important part of chairmanship.

Many meetings take place in advance of a formal board meeting. "People don't go into a board meeting to make a decision. Basically, all sorts of meetings have taken place beforehand in the bar, in the boudoir, with the pal you meet on the plane. The board meeting in a way crystallizes a lot of incoherence into one moment of truth. It is one of those formal last opportunities to say no. At that point people either have to put up or shut up. And in that sense board meetings are a useful kind of braking system on corporate enterprise which is allowed to make decisions without any fear of correction. Board meetings codify what went on because a hell of a lot of things that are done in business are done in an informal way. Many of the people who took the decisions can't remember how the hell they ever took that decision. Board meetings are not institutions of pristine objectivity. Be assured of this, board meetings are political institutions. They are institutions where people fight for things which are directly of interest to them or indirectly of interest. If the board does this and makes that decision there will be peripheral advantages to another company... so people have very complex motives in board meetings.

"I personally consider it a great honour to have lost money with Dr O'Reilly."

"People don't go into a board meeting to make a decision... The board meeting in a way crystallizes a lot of incoherence into one moment of truth."

The chairman can distinguish himself by getting people to talk to the decision so that it is possible to see through to the real reason they are advocating a particular policy."

Tony says that every board is subject to outside pressures. "A board has cliques within it, cliques which actually come on the board not just as a single person but as groups representing other people." Lobbying, preparation and meetings will have taken place beforehand and he illustrates this by talking of his period in Bórd Bainne. "I was Chief Executive of Bórd Bainne when I was twenty-five. I realised there was a tremendous friction between the manufacturers of dairy products, the big co-ops, Ballyclough, Mitchelstown, Killeshandra, and the suppliers of milk. They had antipathetic interests. The milk producers wanted more money for their milk and the manufacturers wanted the cheapest raw material to maximise the margin they could make on the finished product, be it butter, cheese, milk powder or whatever. So you had this inherent contradiction. On the nine-man board there were two government members, four farmers and the members of the manufacturers, one representing cheese, one representing chocolate carob, and the other representing milk powder. Nobody representing butter, funnily enough, which is the biggest product we produced. There were nineteen board meetings per year and each night before the board meeting I would meet in the Stephen's Green Club with the milk producers because (A) they were the preponderant body within the board and (B) they were also the people with whom I identified... there were over one hundred thousand milk producers which, with five or six per family, is six hundred thousand people out of a total population of three million. So it was a mighty constituency in the country. I felt the manufacturers could look after themselves. So I would take the agenda to the Stephen's Green Club and I would sit down with the producer members and we would go through the agenda item by item. There would have been items in which they had no interest. But items relating to subsidy and items relating to investment were of absolutely crucial importance to them. Items relating to the milk levy which we levied on them reduced their return. So I would go through all of that and prepare them so that the next day they, being less professional than the manufacturers or the government representatives, would be able to compete at board level."

Tony says that there are board meetings at which he is relatively apathetic. "I think if I was honest I would say that my interest in decision making is in direct proportion to my ownership of the company. If I own 30% of Independent Newspapers I am hugely concerned about the ethics of the decision making but I don't feel any particular personalised concern about the decision of a board in which I have no stake. It is very hard to have a level of commitment to a business if you don't have a sense of ownership in it. Now, I do not denigrate outside directors *per se,* as a group. I just simply say that the level of passion, of commitment, of understanding they have about a business must be less because they are getting a relatively minor economic return on their time, compared to somebody who owns 10% of the business and whose entire career and whose entire finances are tied up in it. I have proven this to my satisfaction. So I have reached a point in my life where I would not be prepared to be a director of any company, other than charitable ones, where I have not got a major equity in the company. The last board I got off was the Washington Post. And I have been on the boards of Mobil Oil, Bankers Trust, the General Electric Corporation. I took the positions because they were an achievement. They were the ladder climbing devices in the process of achieving a public face on the American continent. And they were prestigious. But once I got inside the door, once I began to understand the process, then I began to understand the enormous toll on my time. The one truly sacred resource you and I have is time. It is inelastic; we are not getting any younger and we all have to maximise this for leisure, for pleasure and for effectiveness." Tony gives 10% of his time each year to the Ireland Fund.

On the issue of the same person being both chairman and chief executive, Tony says "well, being both

" I think if I was honest I would say that my interest in decision making is in direct proportion to my ownership of the company."

130

"The Americans have a sign which is called 'time out'. If you ever see American football matches people do this and it is great."

myself I find it entirely agreeable. I agree with myself most of the time. The problem with Cadbury is that much of Cadbury is entirely laudable and, in an objective sense, Cadbury addresses the custodial aspects of business. A company that might do very well by Cadbury might do awfully badly in the stock market. And if you were asked which is best, a company that is impeccably organised and run *à la* Cadbury but has a limping performance or a company with a megalomaniac chairman who falls drunk on the floor half way through each board meeting but has a stroke of genius and gets results, the shareholders will say 'we will avert our gaze and pick Fred the drunk…'. Now, I am dramatising the situation…"

Tony rarely takes a vote at meetings but would do so if the occasion demanded it and there are, he says, times when people should be allowed to register their vote. Occasionally he would defer taking a decision. "If you have a very big financial stake in a company you will obviously want to let everyone articulate their case. If there are two alternatives and the case against the one you believe in is a strong one, probably the best thing to do is to defer the issue. Then get a third, objective, McKinsey type review. You get Price Waterhouse in to have an objective outsider analysis, consider it again and say 'lets defer this to the next meeting'. The Americans have a sign which is called 'time out'. If you ever see American football matches people do this and it is great. 'Time out' means time to think, time to reflect, time to analyse and I would call for 'time out' at a meeting. This happens when there is a major issue. Major capital investments of an irreversible nature. If we decided to build a plant which is going to be there for a hundred years… this is one you want to take a lot of time to think about."

Tony says that meetings can often be at an impasse for a great number of reasons but, if there are good people who are well informed and who have absolutely contrary points of view, eventually a consensus will emerge. "And if the other people feel extremely strongly that the company is taking the wrong decision, in my view it is incumbent on them to resign. I disagreed with the trading policies of one of the boards I was on. I felt the trading policies were extremely speculative in certain areas and I felt uncomfortable as a member of the board sharing responsibility and liability. I couldn't subscribe to the policy of the company. So I resigned. I think directors should do that more frequently."

Tony recalled the first time he chaired a meeting. It was of the junior cup team at Belvedere College when he was aged fourteen. He was not nervous because his mind was on the forthcoming match against Blackrock College. "I always remember the famous moment when Fr Kerr said to me, 'I feel, my child, I have to tell you that your parents are not married'. He thought this was the biggest deal in the world. I said 'what do you expect me to do about that Father?' And he said 'well, far be it from me to tell you what to do. I just felt I should inform you about this remarkable fact'. I remember my first reaction was 'Jesus, we have got a match against Blackrock next week and if he thinks that fact about my parents is as important as the game in Blackrock he has got another think coming to him'."

Tony describes a poor chairman as one who is a timeserver, is inattentive and lacking in application. "They don't really want confrontation. They have a streak of pusillanimity and they are not prepared to take the bull by the horns. Being a chairman of a great enterprise is a great honour but it should be an honour you take on your own terms. And when your sell by date has arrived..."

He admits that he is sometimes under-prepared for a meeting. "A lot of people do their preparation at the board meeting. A lot of chairmen, if they are honest, will confess to that. The pressure I am under, because of the enormous span of interests I have, is so great that I often find myself under-prepared and have to learn quickly at the meeting..." Effective chairmen, he says, have clarity of mind, simplicity in directness and purpose, "and the capacity to reconcile in a relatively reasonable, humane and humorous way irreconcilable differences without there being acute personal friction at boardroom level."

Dr A.J.F. O'Reilly is Chairman, President and Chief Executive Officer of H.J. Heinz Company. He is also non-executive Chairman of Fitzwilton plc, non-executive Chairman of Independent Newspapers plc, Director of the New York Stock Exchange and of Georgetown University. A world class sportsman Dr O'Reilly played rugby for Ireland twenty-nine times and for the British and Irish 'Lions' team ten times. Active in many cultural and charitable organisations, he is Chairman of The Ireland Funds of the US, Canada, Great Britain, Australia, France, Germany and New Zealand. A Life Fellow of the Irish Management Institute, he has been the recipient of many honours and awards from Irish, British, American and Australian universities.

Chapter 24

An Taoiseach, Albert Reynolds, TD

THE TAOISEACH chairs the most powerful committee in the land and models himself on the late Sean Lemass whose posthumous portrait by Tom Ryan hangs in his office in Government Buildings. "Look up over the mantlepiece. I'd describe my style as brisk and businesslike, like that man up there. From what I know of him, from reading about him, that was his style. He kept it short, sharp and well-focused. He was all about making decisions. Give everybody a fair hearing. At the end of the day pull all the strands together and make decisions. That was his style and I regard that as my style."

The Government's business is, he says, the nation's business and it has to take a wide set of interests into consideration such as pressure groups, trade unions, and business lobbies. "A government meeting has to have a much wider focus than a business meeting where it is about profitability, about strategy, about bottom line. It is a different style. There are so many elements you have to take into account. You have fourteen colleagues around the table all coming from different departments with different inputs into government policy and government decisions. Consequently, as chairman, you have to radiate a sense of fair play across the board and at the same time make sure the contributions are not long-winded but in focus."

His way of dealing with long-winded contributors is to summarise their points for them before they get going. "I know what you are getting at. Here is the point you are making…" He says that a fine balance has to be struck between being patient and dictatorial.

The Taoiseach has never taken a vote in cabinet. He works towards consensus and always gets through the business in the allocated two to two and a half hours. He makes his ministers adhere to the agenda. They do not have an Any Other Business session but they would discuss items of interest either before the meeting starts or after it closes. These might be pressing national issues or something which had occurred the evening before and would not be part of the set agenda. If consensus does not emerge at a meeting the Taoiseach would have bi-lateral meetings between ministers or between a number of ministers and himself. "If you are not going to finalise a particular item on the day because of deeply held views or deep-rooted principles you just leave it there and come back to it the following day but in the meantime you have bi-lateral meetings. I tend not to have a vote but try to bring people with me because everybody subscribes to government policy and there is no point in dividing friends. We are all colleagues around the table. I don't believe in dividing them by votes. I don't think it is good." He believes that voting could be divisive in a coalition government where the chairman has a majority in his own party. "If you set out on the road of taking votes I think the Government will clearly and fairly quickly show instability because people could say 'what's the point of going to a meeting if he has the majority?' It's not a good way to run a meeting."

Chairing a coalition cabinet meeting involves being very sensitive to the different points of view and people must feel a sense of fair play. "What cleared the way for good cabinet meetings was the amount of preparatory work put into the formation of the Government. We had two policy documents, we married the two of them by discussion and by negotiation. We set out a Programme for Government and that's been the guiding parameter of the Government and its activities for the period of government. So consequently a lot of positions are pre-determined. We operate within that guideline. That has been very successful in the present Government. The work we have done before has stood to us. You do a lot more preparatory work in a coalition than you would in a single party government."

The Taoiseach is also experienced at chairing meetings abroad. For these, he studies in advance the people who will be at the meeting. He is then familiar with their styles and the way they will present their views. "There is a lot more homework to be done for these meetings. You have to read the material and carry it with you into the meeting. There will be twelve different nationalities around the table

The Taoiseach has never taken a vote in cabinet.

Chairing a coalition cabinet meeting involves being very sensitive to the different points of view and people must feel a sense of fair play.

and what is important to one will not be important to another. So you have to know exactly where they are all coming from and try to pull things together. You need to display an awful lot of skill and an awful lot of patience. But I think Irish people tend to be good at this. We have always had very successful presidencies in Ireland. We put a lot of work into it and we take nothing for granted. You try to develop personal relationships throughout the period and then, when it comes to your turn to chair, you have these relationships developed. You can rely on them to help you out in difficulties. You always need someone around the table to lead at a particular point, to prompt."

The Taoiseach believes that the fact that the Irish are a small nation is an advantage when chairing in Europe. "The larger nations don't see us as having the same vested interest as some of their other colleagues. We don't have the same hidden agenda as larger nations might have. Although, I have to say, on very large issues you need to have the support of some of the heavyweights. They are able to command more muscle and power."

He says that he sees no harm at all, at home or abroad, in lobbying people before a meeting. He regards it as part of having the homework done.

He regards Chancellor Kohl as a good chairman and there is a lot of respect for him. "Despite the fact that Germany is a powerful nation he will still give everybody around the table the opportunity to get their point across. President Mitterand has a lovely, princely style. Very French and stylish approach. He philosophises a lot. He has a totally different style to Chancellor Kohl but both are very effective in their own way."

Mr. Reynolds also has experience of chairing commercial organisations and at these he says the chair can be much more sharply focused. "The directors are there for one reason and for one reason only, that is to try to make the company successful. The business of a company will be concerned with bottom line, with profits, whereas in government it is a much wider focus. It involves all aspects of human life, it involves society out there, it involves social issues. In a commercial company you would probably have more votes around the table. There is an impression that some chairmen in the commercial world are very dictatorial." He says that if you are the majority shareholder and chair the company's business you can afford to be a little more authoritative. "At shareholders' meetings you can afford to be a bit more dictatorial but you cannot be dictatorial at a cabinet meeting."

He believes that being a good judge of people is an important quality in a chairman. Authority is a skill and he says this comes with experience. "You develop it after a while. You want to get through the agenda and this will be appreciated. When you exercise your authority to draw all the different views together, to deliver a decision – and at the end of the day I have to make the judgement between people – there will very shortly develop a recognition that they have to respect that authority."

Albert Reynolds was elected Taoiseach (Prime Minister of Ireland) on Tuesday 11 February 1992. First elected to Dáil Eireann in 1977, he had been active in local politics as a member of Longford County Council from 1975 to 1979. He was Minister for Industry and Energy in the Fianna Fáil Government of March-December 1982, having served as Minister for Posts and Telegraphs and Minister for Transport from 1979 to 1981; Minister for Industry and Commerce 1987; Minister for Finance 1988; Minister for Finance 1989 to 1991. Elected Leader of Fianna Fail in February 1992. Formerly company director of his family business C & D Foods, pet food manufacturers.

Chapter 25

Dr Michael Smurfit

MICHAEL SMURFIT was a mature thirty-one years old before he ever chaired a meeting. At an Annual General Meeting of the company his father resigned. "My father got up and said 'my son has got the educational background and training and is better capable of running this business than I am and I hereby resign'. And he went off for a six month cruise." At the next board meeting Michael was in the chair and admits to being apprehensive but learned from the secretary of the company what the rules and regulations were. At that stage he did not give much thought to his style of chairing. "No, that developed later on. As the business got bigger I developed my own way of operating. I have a very specific way of running my business. I don't think anyone else does it the same way. I am not saying it is better or worse, it is just what I know. I believe in having few board meetings. I believe in having regular dinners with the board, both personally and collegially. Before a meeting we discuss a lot of issues over dinner in a relaxed atmosphere. Or board members will come to me about different issues. For example, if we want a new colleague, we won't do that at a board meeting. We will chat about it around the office, then go away and think about it and maybe meet some other people. We'll cover up by talking about three or four different people but really we are interested in only one." By the time he goes to his board with a project all his management group are in agreement with it. "Unless we can agree amongst ourselves, there is no point in going to the board. At the end of the day, however, particularly in take-overs, particularly in strategic developments, it comes down to the view of one person. The board look around the table, the management look around the table, the numbers are there but they don't tell you anything. It is the one entrepreneurial view that says, 'guys, we are going to make it work,' that swings the decisions. And that is unfortunately, or fortunately, what I have had to do all my life."

"People who serve on an important board like here are not 'yes-men'."

"One board I was on always had a dove side. Two people who, I always knew, no matter what, would run for a safe haven. 'It can't be done, it wouldn't work, it's too expensive'. And then on the other side, I have always had a couple of hawks who would go for it no matter if the price was ten times the value of it. And then you have the middle of the roaders who want to hear the issues." Michael believes in building up a strong personal bond with each board member. He gets to know them personally on a one to one basis by having lunch or dinner with them "just making sure you know all the people you are dealing with. I suppose I have had four dinners in my home in Monte Carlo in the five years I have been there. I am out every night of the week. It is my life."

In Michael's view the chairman is the focal point of a company, the effective leader and everything else stems from him. "An effective chairman must be knowledgeable about the business, so he must understand what he is talking about. He must know the organisation he is working with. He must have a character which can blend the different talents on the board. Because boards which are effective are those which argue about the issues. People who serve on an important board like ours are not 'yes men'. They are perceptive people and the chairman has to be able to blend all those talents, harness the cultures, the different backgrounds into a result which is a decision. The board is there to make a decision. Finally, at the end of the day you have to look for a result. You can't just leave things in the air. My observation of some chairmen in the past is that they tend to waffle." His description of a poor chairman is one who tries to please everybody. "This is the single biggest mistake a chairman can make. It's called a soft option. A soft option in life is to have a nice collegiate board where everybody agrees with everybody but nothing happens. No result. I found in the semi-state sector where I had a number of important roles over the years, as Chairman of Telecom Eireann and of the Racing Board, that the chairman is a catalyst and if you don't have a strong, active, knowledgeable chairman you won't have a strong, active organisation. So it is vital, in my view, to have a strong chairman." Michael accepted the chairmanship in these semi-state bodies only on the basis that they were going to be run as commercial organisations. "So I ran them during my period no differently from the way I run the Smurfit organisation. I was profit and loss oriented and made the management P and L oriented. They had to be customer oriented, and the fact that they were a monopoly didn't matter a damn. We had to give our customers the same sort of quality and service we gave them in Smurfits. The extraction of dividends from Telecom was a very contentious issue from early on, as the company had a huge debt, an enormous debt and the state wanted, in my view, to fell the tree before the tree was giving fruit."

During his twelve years as chairman of Telecom Eireann there was no occasion on which the board split. "If I got to an impasse on an issue I would put it on the agenda for the next meeting and say 'let's all go away and think about this. We now know what the issues are and let's see if we can find common cause because we are here to come up with a result and an effective one'. I didn't want a split board particularly since Telecom Eireann was in its formative years and we were very much feeling our way. We were a young sapling but effectively a very large tree. We started with twenty-one thousand employees and went down to fourteen thousand. That was a big move without a strike. So we harnessed the talents on the board. I work on the philosophy, which is well known here in Smurfits, problem, solution, result. You will not get a result until you know what the problem is. So you must identify the problem. We had employee elected directors on the board which was a tremendous learning time for me. Notice the words I use, employee elected directors, not worker directors. I said to them 'we are all worker directors. You are elected by the employees so therefore you are employee elected directors. You will be treated no differently than any other director. And the first thing you will do is to go around the organisation and go abroad and visit different places and see how we work and learn about how a board works.' So we trained them. And what we learned from them was tremendous. They knew an awful lot about the heart of the organisation. They were right down in the bowels of it. So, when they came up with a view, I would listen very carefully to that because it

"...the state wanted, in my opinion, to fell the tree before the tree was giving fruit."

"No matter who it was as chairman if he was going to be a crook, he was going to be a crook…"

was the balance against the management. My management were telling me one thing and these people were saying 'you know, Boss, that's not the way it is'. Morale is great. Morale is terrible. Who would I believe? I believed someone I trusted to know the position as against, say, the chief executive who may have thought he knew the position. But he would only get it from his managers. An employee elected director who worked with thousands of people and knew them was a tremendous help."

There are no employee elected directors in Smurfits at the moment whereas in Telecom Eireann he was obliged to have them "and so many females and so on and so forth. I am not obliged in this organisation to have them but it is moving that way. The next directive in the European Union will require an election process."

Michael does not believe in splitting the roles of the chairman and the chief executive and in his view this does not enhance the development of the company. "In fact, I firmly think the opposite. In America they don't do it. In well-run, well-structured businesses there are committees, such as a compensation committee, and solid financial controls. Things like Maxwell did in the UK are an aberration. No matter who it was as chairman, if he was going to be a crook, he was going to be a crook and the same applies in this organisation. If one of my chaps down there is going to be a crook there is nothing I can do to stop him and it will take some time before we find out and the damage will be done. Splitting the responsibilities between the chairman and the chief executive is not a valid argument at all. I don't think it has stood up under any close scrutiny. And, I'm not going to work for anybody."

At Smurfit board meetings Michael would very rarely put something to a vote. "I have a more or less fixed rule. If one director is against something we won't do it. Because of the way I run the boards, if I cannot persuade somebody with my personality and my ability and if that person felt very strongly about an issue I would take that very seriously. So I would not look upon the fact that nine people agreed with me. I would look at the one person who didn't and try to understand him. If he felt very strongly about something I would probably go along with his view."

In the US Michael finds that board meetings are very professional and last less long than those in Europe. It is not uncommon to find a chairman/chief executive on several different boards including universities. They often use the telephone for conference calls. "In fact, we have had a number of these ourselves. Everybody is just on the phone. We discuss issues. Something is proposed and seconded and then approved. I think that here in Smurfits we have modelled ourselves on American boards rather than on European boards. They have very sophisticated committee systems and they are very much crisper. The big boards have some very important chief executives on them and they don't suffer fools gladly. When someone comes in to a presentation it is bang, bang, bang. They want the issues sharp, precise, clear. They want the general counsel to come in with the legal issues and they want to know bang bang bang. They do not have a full day to discuss them."

For Michael the worst meeting in his life was the one at which he informed his colleagues in Telecom Eireann that he was resigning. "The Taoiseach announced that he felt I should step aside for a period as Chairman of Telecom Eireann. Now he clearly had not thought about it carefully enough. You could not step aside from a semi-state company as large as Telecom Eireann for a year. It just wasn't on. Therefore, in effect he really was saying 'either you resign or I will fire you'. That was the issue as I saw it . That was a disgraceful thing to happen. There was no impropriety by myself. I would have preferred it if he had fired me. And then I would have taken him on publicly. That was my approach. I was so goddam mad. But the Smurfit board controls my time and I served on Telecom Eireann because they allowed me to. They said that 'no way should you step aside, and no way can he fire you, so you should resign'. They were probably right. When I went to Telecom Eireann and informed them of my decision it was a very emotional moment. I was very saddened by it. I had worked with these people for twelve years. I was very upset because it was the first time in my life I had been emotional at a board meeting. I was hurt by what had happened. The press were having a field

"I suppose I have had four dinners in my home in Monte Carlo in the five years I have been there."

day because they thought there was some scandal. There never was a scandal. There was a lot of shouting and roaring about nothing. But that was the time that was in it. I put it behind me immediately. I am one of those people who has been able to get over adversity very quickly. I closed the book."

Michael does not remember ever missing a board meeting or being late for one. He says that it is important for the chairman to create a positive atmosphere at a meeting and that this helps it along. "You've got to have a certain amount of laughter. If you don't have a sense of humour, you don't have a life. The chairman is running the meeting, he's got the agenda. If he is in a sour, foul humour, that will permeate the meeting. I've sometimes been very tired after long trips and it can have a negative result because you dampen the mood of the meeting. You've got to keep yourself chirpy, alive and I do not allow my dark, inner pain…"

Dr Michael Smurfit is Chairman and Chief Executive Officer of Jefferson Smurfit Group plc. He is also Director of Jefferson Smurfit Corporation; Container Corporation of America and SIBV/MS Holdings, Inc. He joined Jefferson Smurfit & Sons Ltd in 1955 and left to form Jefferson Smurfit Packaging Limited in Lancashire in 1961. He rejoined Jefferson Smurfit Group as a Director in 1964 becoming Joint Managing Director in 1967. He was appointed Deputy Chairman in 1969 and became Chairman and Chief Executive in 1977. In 1979 he became Chairman of the Interim Telecommunications Board which subsequently became Telecom Eireann and served until September 1991. He was Chairman of The Racing Board from 1985 until 1990. He is a Fellow of the International Academy of Management; conferred with Honorary Doctorate of Laws Trinity College Dublin; NUI; University of Scranton, Pennsylvania; Babson College, Boston; Honorary Doctor of Engineering, University of Missouri; Honorary Irish Consul Monaco. He has been awarded the Cross and Star of a Grand Officer of Merit of the Knightly Order Pro Merito Melitensi; Commendatore of the Order of Merit of the Italian Republic; Orden Francisco de Miranda, Venezuela; Order Al Merito Nacional, Colombia; Legion d'Honneur, France; Cross of Merit of the Holy Sepulchre of Jerusalem.

Chapter 26

Peter Sutherland

WHEN PETER SUTHERLAND chaired the final stages of the Uruguay round of the GATT negotiations he was in the chair on one day for seventeen hours. Negotiations had gone on for seven years and they now had a firm deadline. One hundred and twenty countries participated in the discussions with about twenty to thirty of these being major players. During the last ten days of meetings Peter averaged three to four hours sleep. "If we didn't finish by 15 December the negotiations failed. At one o'clock on that day I had a phone call from a Prime Minister in Latin America to say he was going to pull the plug on the round even though we had reached agreement the previous night – something had been done improperly by another party and he was enraged by this as were a number of others. We solved the problem at the last moment and finished on time. The agreement consisted in volume terms of 22,000 pages and on goods alone having an immediate impact on the world economy of two hundred additional trades to the value of over 250 billion dollars a year, worldwide. So we were not talking about a simple issue. It was extremely tense."

Peter says that he had no ideological position. He wanted to get an agreement by the deadline. "As Chairman of the Trade Negotiations Committee and Director General of GATT, I said constantly that I would personally broker an agreement. I was prepared to say that black was white if that would get an agreement. I didn't give a damn. I saw my role as being very simple, no position on anything, get an agreement by hook or by crook, by whatever means necessary, fair rather than foul I hope, but having a bit of humour as well. Certainly, it was very tough and one had to be tough publicly as well, particularly with the big boys, but I don't think they took it badly. The pressure was terrible – I wouldn't do it again."

He believed that if the Uruguay round failed, the world would move into a disastrous round of conflict. "I believed passionately in one thing. I believed, as the former Singapore Prime Minister Lee Kuan Yew did also, that there would be a war within ten years as a result of failure. So I was prepared to do almost anything. I travelled around the world constantly. My interest was in getting a decision because this meant then that we would have a multi-lateral agreement on which trade could develop and I didn't care what the hell it contained."

Speaking of meetings in general, Peter says that some meetings require consensus and that others do not. He picks out impartiality and vision as two important qualities or characteristics in a chair. He also stresses the value of a little humour. "A chairman has to impart an air of impartiality and yet, at the same time, there has to be a clear idea in his mind as to the direction he wants the meeting to take. I think that they are not incompatible. In other words, it is possible to have a vision, an idea in advance of the direction one would like the meeting to take. Also, I think it is very important, frankly, to have a sense of humour. If you don't have a sense of humour as a chairman the meeting can become much more fractious than it otherwise might be. The introduction of an element of humour can often bring about a situation where tensions can evaporate very rapidly. Particularly at high level meetings humour is important. Because at these meetings people are inclined to be more portentous, more pompous and self righteous – I think humour is extremely important."

A chairman also needs to be decisive at the vital moment and must not allow a discussion to go on for too long in a desperate effort to reach consensus. "The futile search for consensus is the most debilitating factor in the running of meetings. If one searches for a consensus that is never going to arrive and one keeps talking on a subject up and down, round and round, over and over again, even though it is quite obvious that a consensus is not attainable, this ends up making people frustrated and more difficult rather than less difficult. One has seen this in different situations, in government, where one could argue and discuss for hours and hours and hours."

"…I said constantly that I would personally broker an agreement. I was prepared to say that black was white if that would get an agreement. I didn't give a damn."

"The futile search for consensus is the most debilitating factor in the running of meetings."

Peter says the best way to handle an impasse situation is to let the minority at a meeting hear the extent of the opposition from the majority and to allow the most articulate and forceful of them to say their piece. Then the minority can reply and after that he would advise an adjournment period. "I think this is rather better than trying to force the discussion on to a stage where the parties almost come to blows. When they reflect on it, the minority will realise they are getting nowhere and they will have to compromise. The time has to come when the chairman, the Taoiseach, the president, the director general or whoever simply says 'right, we are going to conclude the discussion here because we are not going to reach agreement and talking at each other isn't the way to achieve it'." In this impasse situation he says it is important for the chairman to recognise that there is likely to be an impasse before the meeting gets under way. Also, he should have devised, preferably in advance of the meeting, a strategy on how to deal with the impasse. "It is very bad and wrong for a chairman to go to a meeting and not be able to foretell accurately what is going to happen at the meeting. Because if you don't know what is going to happen and if you don't have a broad idea as to the position people are going to take on different issues you won't be able to handle it. If your contacts with the people are adequate you will know what their positions are going to be and you should then be able to play the meeting. You should not allow people to dig themselves into a hole unnecessarily because it then becomes more difficult to find the compromise to get them out of it. In the impasse situation the chairman has to find, if it is findable, the compromise that is the probable solution to the problem. And then he has to decide whether it is better that he should float it as chairman or use another member to float it for him. Normally it is better to allow some time to elapse, in order for the minority to realise they are isolated, before having a smaller meeting to seek a solution. Whatever step you next take to find a mechanism around the blockage has to be sensitive to the bruised ego of the person who has to compromise. So one has to find a way of doing it which doesn't offend the sensibilities of the person who has to give in on the argument. Face is not merely a concern for orientals. It is a concern for everybody and everybody has their sensitivities, particularly when they believe they are right."

Peter recalls his first meeting as the Irish Commissioner in the EC when Jacques Delors was President. Previously, votes had not been taken at these meetings. The Commissioner for Agriculture said he wanted to have a number of habilitations passed and Delors agreed to this suggestion. "Nobody said anything. It was the first time we met as a Commission and I put up my hand and said that I didn't agree. First of all, I didn't know what the word habilitation meant. I did not know what they were talking about and I certainly wasn't going to agree to anybody getting a power to take decisions on subjects which had not been defined for me and which the Commission would never see or hear anything about. Delors said to me that I was being extremely unreasonable and that he understood that this was always done at a first Commission meeting. But, I said, I had no notice of this and would not agree to it. I suggested that we adjourn for a week or if he wanted to push it that far that a vote be taken. So the vote was taken and I was defeated by seven to five as I recall it, but the fact that I got five votes in the particular circumstances was not bad. It was a very tense meeting and it was a very unfortunate beginning to a Commission. In fact, Delors and I subsequently became very good friends, but it created a precedent. After that Delors said 'look, if we are ever going to do business in this place, if we look for consensus the whole time we will never get agreement or it will be the worst possible agreement because it will be the lowest common denominator. So we have to accept the need for votes.' Later, if someone was beaten in a vote, it didn't make a big difference but on that first day it was pretty terrible and traumatic. Afterwards I felt gravely wounded."

Peter became Chairman of Allied Irish Banks in 1989, never having served on any board before. He believes that on such boards there should be a majority of non-executive directors in order to provide balance. "The non-executive chairman has a delicate role to play. On the one hand one is naturally closer to the executives than the other non-executive directors.

"It is very bad and wrong for a chairman to go to a meeting and not be able to foretell accurately what is going to happen at the meeting."

"Face is not merely a concern for orientals. It is a concern for everybody..."

One is involved two or three days a week and in constant contact with policies as they are being prepared for presentation to the board. On the other hand, one has to remain impartial as chairman. The idea of having a non-executive chairman is, in a sense, to provide protection for the shareholders' interests. One does not get into automatic rubber stamping policies which are coming through from the executives. Now, in the vast majority of cases, it should not arise that the non-executives would take a view contrary to that proposed to them by the executives. But that power has to be there and from time to time it has to be exercised. Sometimes executives can become too close, too wedded to a theory or to a proposition. They get over involved or so committed to it by virtue of positions they have taken in the past that they can't extract themselves. But it should not get to a stage where it is confrontational, and in my experience it doesn't. Sometimes there are difficulties. When I was on the board of British Petroleum the chairman was relieved of his position. The non-executives decided that there should be a change. Hard decisions, particularly about someone one likes, are difficult to take. But sometimes they are taken."

An effective chairman has to be a good communicator and Peter thinks that Irish people have a natural ability in this area. "A fundamental attribute of a chairman is communication. And I don't mean the capacity to articulate but the capacity to communicate with people in a sympathetic way. You have to be able to respond to people, to talk to people, to get on with people. In the international forum being Irish is a considerable advantage because one is not typecast as being either from the developed world or the developing world. Coming from a small country, which I think is generally quite popular, one doesn't have a negative image. Virtually every major country in Europe has historic images, associated with it by its neighbours, which create tensions. It is only the small and inoffensive which can avoid that. Irish people don't see themselves as coming from any particular class. It doesn't create any difficulty for them to go into a pub, sit down and talk to anybody. Now that is an unusual thing and it gives you a tremendous ability to communicate."

Being pro-active is part of being an effective chairman and Peter engages in what he describes as "pre-cooking". He goes into a meeting with a clear idea of the way he would like it to go. "Well, rightly or wrongly, I'm afraid I normally go into a meeting knowing what I want to come out with but not to the extent that I would steamroll over people. In private discussions before a meeting you should not create cabals or groups. What you say to one person you should be prepared to say to the whole lot of them because otherwise you lose the necessary impartiality. But you don't go blind into a meeting without an idea of what people are actually going to say or do. You have to be pro-active. If you aren't, if you just allow meetings to take place without any pre-cooking or preparation, you are walking into trouble."

Whether a chairman should be an arbiter or leader is a difficult question and he says that he believes they have to be a bit of both.

"I do not believe it is a good thing for a chairman to be so removed from the issues that he cannot provide leadership at the end of the day. Arbitration is needed at the initial phase but I think that a chairman who doesn't have a clear idea of where he is going is not doing a good job."

If he found there was a clear majority in favour of a conclusion with which he was not happy he says that he would "roll on with it". "As chairman, you shouldn't try to impose your view or use your position in any way to distort that conclusion. Decisions have been taken where I personally would have taken a different one and, as chairman, I hope I facilitated those decisions being taken. At a certain stage I recognised that there was a clear view contrary to mine even though one or two people might have agreed with me. So I went to them and said 'look, it's quite clear that our view is not the general one so we must revise and concede', and we did." In these circumstances he would not use a tactic such as looking for more information in order to postpone the decision. "No, you can't do that. That is the inhibition of being chairman. I suppose as an ordinary member of a committee or board you can play games and try to stop a decision being taken because you feel so passionately about something. But I certainly don't

"…on that first day it was pretty terrible and traumatic. Afterwards I felt gravely wounded."

think a chairman should use his power to adjourn a discussion for the purpose of obstructing the majority view from prevailing. In fact, I think you would have to lean over backwards not to do that."

With all his vast experience on the Irish, European and world stages, Peter's advice to a chairman is to be cautious. "I have learned not to become wedded to any particular view until I have heard the whole thing through. Because you often find that no matter how strongly you think you are right, that you are not. And therefore it is the delicate combination of flexibility with principle that is the vital thing. Flexibility has to be combined with your fundamental beliefs in certain things. Chairing is a skill. Assuming that you understand the concepts you are dealing with, I don't think it makes much difference whether you are chairing a golf club, a tennis club, a business, a commission or whatever."

He stresses the need for a chairman to get to know the people he is leading really well. "Spend a great deal of time communicating with the other people who are involved in the issue on a bi-lateral basis. Good relationships are the most important thing of all. Spend an enormous amount of time getting to know everybody in the group. If people don't know you, they will dislike you. Or they may feel you are arrogant or this or that. The only way to overcome that is by having a personal relationship with them. Very few people know other people. One creates all sorts of illusions about other people. That, I think, is the most obvious lesson in life."

Peter Sutherland is Director General of GATT, having officially assumed his duties on 1 July 1993. During the period from 1989 to 1993 he was Chairman of Allied Irish Banks and was a member of the boards of a number of other companies. From 1969 to 1981 he practised at the Bar, and thereafter served as Attorney General of Ireland and as a member of the Council of State until the end of 1984 when he was nominated by the Government a Commissioner of the European Communities. From 1985 to 1989 he served in Brussels as the Commissioner responsible for Competition Policy. During this period his other Commission dossiers were Social Affairs, Education and Relations with the European Parliament. In 1988 he was the first EC Commissioner to receive the Gold Medal of the European Parliament. His other awards include the First European Law Prize (Paris 1988); the Grand Cross of Civil Merit (Spain 1989); the Grand Cross of King Leopold II (Belgium 1989); the New Zealand Commemorative Medal (1990); Chevalier de la Légion d'Honneur (France 1993) and Commandeur du Wissam (Morocco 1994). His publications include the book Premier Janvier 1993 ce qui va changer en Europe.

Chapter 27

Bridín Twist

BRIDÍN TWIST well remembers the first meeting she chaired, which was in 1974. She had been elected President of her guild of the ICA and she describes the experience as "nerve-wracking". From being a member in the audience she now found herself on the "other side of the table" with responsibility for making the meeting work. "I spent time concentrating on myself to keep myself calm and took lots of deep breaths. It is important that the floor doesn't recognise that you are nervous. Every organisation has people in it who tend to be very vocal and who take over the meeting if they see the opportunity." She sees herself as an efficient chair and stresses the need for punctuality. "But I'm a fun person. In our organisation we discuss very serious issues and we are bound to have controversy. If two people are at each other's throats it's good to have a little fun now and again. Humour is important."

Bridín finds that being petite is a disadvantage when in the chair and, in fact, she often stands in order to be visible. "I find that small people have a problem chairing. I really do. Standing on the odd occasion has an impact. I've watched other people who do this. Small people in high positions have a problem. It is easier for tall people."

Guild meetings of the ICA appear to be very well organised by the officers because they have pre-meetings to prepare the agenda and to discuss the issues which will come up. "We are very well structured. This pre-meeting keeps us all well informed and up to date on issues." It also means that she, as Chairwoman, knows the mood of several people going into a meeting and she can call on them to speak if she sees the meeting going off the rails.

While she comes across as a strong-minded woman, Bridín says that a chairwoman should not hold firm views. "A chair should never influence a meeting. You have to be very careful. Strong-minded people with very strong views shouldn't be in the chair because they tend to express their opinion rather than asking people for theirs. You have to be impartial and not let yourself be swayed. If there is a vote and it is very tight the chairwoman will have to give the casting vote and she can't do this if she has previously got carried away on an issue. If you intervene too much and take over the meeting, that to me is not chairing. You have to utilise your people at the meeting, that's what they are there for."

In the ICA, unlike many organisations, votes are frequently taken at their meetings, both in the guilds and at the national level. They find this works well. On policy issues or a change to their constitution a vote is always taken. "We find voting works well. We are very democratic and the minority doesn't feel alienated. Every meeting is prepared for a vote with ballot papers etc. and every delegate guild has the right to send their vote to Council. When in the chair, sometimes you think you have a consensus on an issue and then you hear a strong murmur of dissent. So when that happens we take a vote. And that solves the matter immediately. There is no more controversy."

Bridín is quite firm with people who talk very frequently at meetings. She might say "Mary, you have spoken twice on this subject, now, I would like to hear from X." She says that at every meeting there are people who have very strong views and who are very vocal. "We would do our best to be firm with them. We always have that policy." The other matter on which a chairwoman has to be firm, she says, is dealing with distractions on the floor of a meeting. "If a group of people down in a corner are having a discussion I find that very distracting. It is distracting for the chair but also for the people around the talkers. And, if you are trying to concentrate on something, you start to wonder are they concocting something down there in the corner. So I would say to them 'Mary, perhaps you have a view on this which you would like to share with the rest of us?'"

Bridín believes that chairing meetings is a great confidence builder. In her own case she found that she was much more confident about speaking out at other meetings from the floor once she had the experience of chairing behind her. "You have to be

"I spent time concentrating on myself to keep myself calm and took lots of deep breaths."

"Strong-minded people with very strong views shouldn't be in the chair because they tend to express their opinion rather than asking people for theirs."

confident dealing with a large group of people. You learn a lot about people. And you learn how difficult it is to be on the other side of the table when you are trying to deal with a big number of people." Up to eight hundred delegates attend ICA council meetings.

Bridín goes to many meetings other than the ICA, both in Ireland and abroad. She believes that women at meetings are more businesslike than men. "Women are more punctual and very businesslike. They leave the meeting immediately it is over whereas men would tend to hang around. Men are lingerers. I would also say that men have made their contacts before a meeting, have lobbied for whatever they want to happen at the meeting and fixed the decisions in advance. Women, on the other hand, would listen to the views expressed and make their decisions at the meeting."

Bridín has witnessed much frustration at meetings due to the fact that they were being badly chaired. In this situation, the committee members became very irritated. "On the one hand, you have the very strong-minded chair who intervenes too much and then loses rapport with the audience. Then there is the chairwoman who has not done her homework on the issues on the agenda. Therefore she can't control the meeting. And then you find that the strong-minded people on the floor take over the meeting and this leads to much aggravation. So it is important to get it right."

Bridín Twist is National President of the Irish Countrywomen's Association. She joined the Association in 1977 and, having served at Guild and Federation level, became Vice-Chairman of the Executive Committee and Chairman of the National Development Committee before being elected National President in May 1994. She also represents the organisation at international conferences and is the ICA's delegate on the Confederation of Family Organisations of Europe. A business woman, she is the Vice-Chairman of the Clare County Enterprise Board.

Chapter 20

Arthur Walls

Arthur Walls remembers the first meeting he chaired quite clearly. He was sixteen and it was at a tennis club in Clontarf.

A large, friendly, confident man, he admits to becoming fidgety at meetings chaired by others. He resigned from a state board some time ago because he felt that, with eighteen members all expressing their views, the board was far too large. "I found myself falling asleep", he says, "so I left."

As Chief Executive and Chairman of the board of Clerys, however, he does not make a habit of falling asleep at meetings. Before going to Clerys he worked for twenty-five years as General Manager of Aer Lingus. There he met Michael Dargan whom he quotes as teaching him much about the art of chairmanship.

"Michael said to me 'a good chairman should watch the sheep trials on television. When the sheep are all moving in the right direction the good sheepdog just lies flat and does nothing'. He was right. I have seen many meetings where everything was going along nicely and about to be closed when a chairman makes an ill-considered move and suddenly the sheep are all gone in different directions again. So, the golden rule of chairmanship is if the meeting is moving towards a consensus or towards the conclusion you want, leave it alone. Don't bark suddenly or make a statement which will scatter the sheep again."

"Now, I'm not describing the directors as sheep. I'm describing the opinions as sheep. You have got to get them all into the one pen and close the gate as soon as you have them in. It can be counter-productive to try to summarise. Many television compères have a bad habit of doing this. You can summarise the facts and the conclusions but not the views which have been expressed. Don't try to tell people what they are thinking and remember, in law, minutes are only required to record attendance and decisions."

Arthur says that a skilled chairman should remember and keep referring to the aims of the meeting. A board could, on occasion, simply exchange views or have a discussion on future policy objectives. An annual general meeting, on the other hand, will have explicit motions which have to be got through. "And", he says, "the chairman has to be very tough and even rude sometimes."

Arthur feels that Irish directors are terribly casual about their responsibilities. Often they do not know what is going on in the company. Directors are required to run the company and to run it honestly and the chief executive is the instrument of the directors. "Again and again I read in the papers about people who say that they did not know the company was borrowing money. Well, they should have known. Often a son or daughter is put on a board and they do not know what is going on. The law says that each director must represent the interests of all the shareholders equally."

"This brings me to an important point on which a chairman has to be very careful. For example, if a company is in financial trouble and a bank appoints a director to its board he will often say at a meeting 'I will have to make sure the bank's interest is protected'. Now, that is quite wrong and a chairman should not let him away with it."

He says that directors should ask questions about the company's borrowings, the state of the bank account, the lease of a building. "You are very often thought of as a doddery old nuisance but you have to be firm. Ask the chairman to have a report for the next meeting. Often a chief executive is deliberately economical with information. Everybody likes power. He wants to run the company his way and therefore he tells his board as little as he will get away with."

Arthur says that even at a high level there is much confusion between the duties of the different officers within a company. "There is a funny paradox for the people who own a company, be it a minister or a group of shareholders. They do not have any direct power over the company. Their job is to get the right directors. Their job, in turn, is to get the right chief executive and the chief executive's job is to get the right financial controller. Therefore, when you are promoted from being an executive to a director and from director to chairman you must

"When the sheep are all moving in the right direction the good sheepdog just lies flat and does nothing."

160

*"...the chairman has
to be very tough and
even rude sometimes."*
understand the difference. A director is not simply a senior executive. Unfortunately, an awful lot of people are confused about this and it can lead to real problems."

Arthur says that experience gives a person authority. A chairman needs to exercise control and to do this he or she needs to understand procedure and to have a knowledge of the law on meetings. In his view a poor chairman is one who always tries to get total unanimity. "The worst chairman I ever worked with was too nice. He felt obliged to get unanimity, with the result that the meetings went on for ever. A chairman's job is to say 'right, the consensus of the meeting is to do such and such' and if someone does not agree with you they can challenge you, but normally they won't."

Arthur believes in working by consensus rather than taking a vote. "I do not like counting hands and have only done this on about three occasions in my life. This related to discipline, where we proposed to fire a chief executive, and I had to know where each person stood on the matter. It couldn't be fudged. Otherwise taking the feeling of the meeting is best because losers are always embarrassed and they will go back and press their point rather than appear to be foolish. You need to lead the meeting towards decisions. I don't like to use the word dominate but it is something between leadership and domination."

Another aspect of authority is punctuality and control of time. If the meeting is to finish at 12.00 he says that it should finish at 12.00 and not 12.05. "You do this by looking at your watch at 11.45 and saying 'now, we only have fifteen minutes left, we can stay on this item and defer the following three items to the following meeting'. I think you owe it to people to be careful with their time, particularly part-time directors. They are there for a specific time, they get specific fees. You should not let a meeting over-run. Some chairmen let them go on for ever. People run late for their next appointment, it ruins their day and you lose good board members. You must start the meeting on time. I have, on occasion, started meetings with just myself and the secretary and members came in late sheepishly but next time they'll arrive on time." He believes that 11.00 am is the best time of day for a meeting because it doesn't go on too long, ending usually before lunch.

At an AGM, timing and the order of the agenda are critical. "If the last item on the agenda is the declaration of the dividend, shareholders know that they will not get their cheque until they get to this item. Whereas, if you declare the dividend first, most people will then go home but others will want to stay discussing things all night. Deciding the order of the agenda, even for a routine board meeting, can make a hell of a difference."

Arthur likes the role of chairman because he can control the meeting and the pace of it. He admits to going to a meeting with a clear view of what he wants from it. "In theory, I shouldn't do this but in practice I am human. I will push things. I'll try to get my own way even though I may be doing this subconsciously. I think all chairmen do the same even if they do not admit it. I don't honestly believe anyone is objective about anything." He tends to shoot from the hip which he says is sometimes good and sometimes bad but he doesn't try to change his personality in the chair.

A skilled chairman must have the ability to grasp reports. He also needs to understand what someone is trying to get at. Chairing voluntary organisations is, in his experience, very difficult and requires more charismatic skills. "In a company there is a hierarchy and, at the end of the day, a chairman can say 'I have heard your views and this is the way I think we should go'. In a tennis club if you say that people who are giving their time free take umbrage!"

Arthur Walls is Deputy Chairman Clery & Co. (1941) plc; Chairman of Dublin Crystal Glass Co. Ireland Ltd and of Air Tara Limited (GPA Subsidiary). He is a Director of Guiney & Co. Ltd, and Ryanair Limited. He worked in Aer Lingus from 1947 to 1972 progressing to General Manager, then became Managing Director of RTD (Ryan Group) before becoming Managing Director of Clerys in 1974. He became Deputy Chairman in 1992. He is Chairman of the Stanhope Alcoholic Centre, a Director of Dublin Zoo and of the James Joyce Cultural Centre. He is a Fellow of the Royal Aero. Society and a Fellow of the Chartered Institute of Transport.